IN THE PULP FICTION TRENCHES

MY TUMULTUOUS LITERARY CAREER

LEN LEVINSON

ROUGH
EDGES
PRESS

*To William Kotzwinkle, Lin Carter and Peter McCurtin, who
helped me understand how to write stories.*

*And to Michael Olds, who emphasized the importance of word
order in sentences, and sentence order in paragraphs, and
paragraph order in stories.*

IN THE PULP FICTION TRENCHES

HOW IT ALL BEGAN

As I look back at my literary career, which consists of 86 published novels, I think it all began in 1946 when I was age 11 in the Fifth Grade, John Hannigan Grammar School, New Bedford, Massachusetts.

A teacher named Miss Ribeiro asked students to write essays of our choosing. Some kids wrote about baking cookies with mommy, or fishing excursions to Cuttyhunk with Dad, or taking the bus to Boston to watch the Red Sox play the Yankees at Fenway Park, etc.

My mommy died when I was four and dear old Dad never took me anywhere. So Little Lenny Levinson wrote a science fiction epic about an imaginary trip to the planet Pluto, probably influenced by Buck Rogers, perhaps expressing subliminal desires to escape my somewhat Dickensian childhood.

As I wrote, the classroom seemed to vanish. I sat at the control panel of a sleek, silver space ship hurtling past spinning suns, glowing moons and blazing constellations. While writing, I experienced something I can only describe today as an out-of-body, ecstatic hallucination, evidently the pure joy of self-expression.

I returned to earth, handed in the essay, and expected the usual decent grade. A few days later Miss Ribeiro praised me in front of the class and read the essay aloud, first time I'd been singled out for excellence. Maybe I'll be a writer when I grow up, I thought.

As time passed, it seemed an impractical choice. Everyone said I'd starve to death. I decided to prepare for a realistic career but couldn't determine exactly what it would be.

In 1954, age 19, I joined the Army for the GI Bill, assuming a Bachelor's degree somehow would elevate me to the Middle Class. After mustering out in 1957, I enrolled at Michigan State University, East Lansing, majored in Social Science, received my B.A. in 1961, and travelled to New York City to find a job.

Drifting with the tides, in 1970 I was employed as a press agent at Solters and Sabinson, a show biz publicity agency near Times Square. Our clients at various times included Frank Sinatra, Barbra Streisand, Bob Hope, Dolly Parton, the Beatles, Rolling Stones, Flip Wilson, Ringling Brothers and Barnum and Bailey Circus, Holiday on Ice, Playboy, Caesar's Palace in Las Vegas, numerous Broadway shows and countless movies, among others.

It was at Solters and Sabinson that certain life-transforming events occurred, ultimately convincing me to become a full-time novelist.

Wheels of the cataclysm were set in motion innocuously enough by press agent Jerry Augburn, whose desk jammed beside mine in a large, open office packed with approximately 20 hustling press agents and secretaries.

2

Unusual in that raucous atmosphere, Jerry was a well-mannered WASP from Muncie, Indiana with B.A. in English from Ball State U and Ph.D. from Columbia. Through some trick of fate, he landed in entertainment publicity instead of becoming a professor. Together we represented the New York Playboy Club, and individually worked for other clients.

One day Jerry complained he wasn't feeling well. Soon afterwards he was diagnosed with leukemia, stopped coming to the office, left word he didn't want calls. A few months later, he died around age 35. Intelligent, capable, good guy, husband and father – suddenly gone. Wow.

I never thought much about death until Jerry's passing. According to Hinduism which I studied at the time, death is a normal stage through which all sentient beings pass on journeys to next incarnations. Death surely would carry me away someday as Death had carried away Jerry. Perhaps I'd return as a chimpanzee, fish or possibly a cockroach someone would stomp.

Weeks passed; the office seemed to forget Jerry like he never existed. Jerry's desk was taken over by Jay Russell, press agent in his 50s, who spent his days writing column items.

One night approximately three months after Jerry's demise, Jay and I worked late. I went home around 9pm, leaving him behind. Next morning, I learned that he died of a heart attack the previous night sitting on his home toilet, writing column items. I'm not making this up. That's the story I was told.

After Jay's funeral, I reflected upon Death striking twice at the chair beside mine. Was I next on the hit parade? Meanwhile, the office returned to its usual pressure cooker atmosphere. After a few weeks Jay was forgotten like Jerry.

I was 35 like Jerry, looking down the road at 40. If I died at my desk or on the toilet, unquestionably I too would soon be forgotten by co-workers and clients. What was the point of busting my chops if it meant nothing in the end?

I'm not exaggerating about busting my chops. Competition for clients was ferocious. A press agent was only as good as his last media break. If it didn't break – it never happened. If you didn't produce steady breaks – you were on the street.

Consequently I spent substantial time on the phone asking editors and reporters to run my press releases, interview my clients, and cover my events. All too often they rejected my pleading because they had limited space in their publications, or limited time on their broadcasts, and their phones never stopped ringing from press agents' calls, their mailboxes stuffed daily with press releases.

Gradually it dawned upon me that I was in the wrong job for my personality type. But what on earth was the right job for my personality type?

Since the fifth grade my grandest ambition remained: novelist. In light of Jerry's and Jay's passing, I slowly came to the life-altering realization that I didn't want to kick the bucket without at least attempting to fulfill my highest career aspiration.

I'd already tried writing at home evenings, after working all day in the office, but my mind was too tired. If I wanted to be a novelist, I needed to approach it like a job, first thing in the morning when my mind was clear, no distractions. That meant I'd need to quit my regular job. My savings would support me for around a year. Surely I'd be on the bestseller list by then.

I wasn't totally delusional. I knew that substantial risk including possible homelessness accompanied the novelist's life. I had no family to provide financial assistance or a place to bunk if I hit the skids.

On the other hand, if I played it safe and remained in PR, suppressing frustration and dissatisfaction, I'd probably evolve into a well-pensioned, gray-bearded, ex-PR semi-alcoholic residing comfortably in a West Side co-op, or gated community in Boca Raton, happily married to a former Playboy Bunny.

But the day inevitably would arrive when I'd be flat on my back in a hospital bed, tubes up my nose and jabbing into my arms, on the cusp of Death Itself. And knowing how my mind tends to function, I'd reproach myself viciously for not at least attempting to live my dream, since I was going to die regardless. Why not go for the gold ring of the novelist's life instead of getting put down daily by journalists?

After much meditation on death, heaven, hell, destiny, mendacity and art, I resigned my press agent career and threw my heart and brain cells completely into writing novels. It was the bravest, most consequential and possibly most foolish decision of my life.

You can call me shallow, immature, irresponsible and/or insane, but I never betrayed my ideal. Against the odds, I went on to write those 86 paperback novels, mostly in the high adventure category, about cops, cowboys, soldiers, spies, cab drivers, race car drivers, ordinary individuals seeking justice in an unjust world, and other lunatics, but never had a hit. Sometimes I wondered if I'd chosen the wrong profession. But it didn't seem like a choice. Instead, it seemed more of a deep-rooted compulsion to tell stories and express myself.

At least I needn't torment myself on my deathbed for not attempting to become a novelist.

Perhaps the novelist's life is its own reward. And punishment.

MY PSEUDONYMS

LET ME ANSWER ONE BIG QUESTION RIGHT AWAY. PEOPLE often ask why I've used so many pseudonyms. Below are the reasons:

My first published novel was hard core erotica. Writers traditionally use pseudonyms for hard core erotica and so did I.

Then I wrote novels in series developed in-house by publishing companies. All writers who worked on the series used a name invented by the publisher. For example, all writers in the *Sharpshooter* series published by Belmont-Tower used the pseudonym *Bruno Rossi*.

Finally I wrote a standalone novel called *Operation Perfidia* published by Warner, and could use my real name but decided not to because I thought the novel might be considered politically controversial, and might upset someone who might want to shoot me. Or if the novel made lots of money, someone might want to kidnap my daughter. So I chose a pseudonym *Leonard Jordan*, my first and middle names. I subsequently used *Leonard Jordan* for all my standalone novels.

I also wrote standalone novels at the request of publishers and used pseudonyms invented by them or occasionally invented by me. For example, I became *Cynthia Wilkerson* for two novels written from women's points of view.

Then I started developing and writing my own series. The first was a James Bond-type spy thriller series called *Butler*. The contract stipulated that the publisher could hire other writers for the series if I was busy with other obligations, because the publisher wanted the same author's name for the sake of consistency. I didn't want anyone else using my *Leonard Jordan* so we settled on *Philip Kirk*. This same basic arrangement was used for all other series that I developed, incorporating a variety of pseudonyms.

My last three novels were published under my real name, Len Levinson. Many of my novels have been republished as ebooks and as paperbacks also by Len Levinson. I'm not worried about assassination or kidnapping anymore, although perhaps I should be.

MY FIRST PUBLISHED NOVEL

My FIRST PUBLISHED NOVEL WAS HARD CORE XXX-RATED erotica, or in other words a dirty book.

I never intended to write a dirty book when first I decided to become a novelist. My goal was to play in the same league as Norman Mailer, Saul Bellow, John Cheever, Philip Roth, Bernard Malamud and John Updike, among other contemporary American writers of quality literature.

Why did I write a dirty book?

Out of desperation – why else? Here's how it happened.

I quit my PR job to become a full-time writer in 1971 and completed my first novel that year. I began the novel in 1965 when I still had a job. It was quality literature in my opinion, and good enough to get me a wonderful literary agent, Elaine Markson, but she was unable to make a sale. (I will discuss this novel in greater detail later.)

I ran out of money and had to take whatever job I could find. Like many other artsy types living in New

York City in those days, I became a cabdriver, in my case on the night shift 4pm to 4am. This was during the 1970s when cab driving was an extremely dangerous profession.

It also was a fascinating profession inspiring me to write my second novel, about a cabdriver. I drove three nights per week, wrote four nights, and slept during days like a vampire. I finally completed the taxicab novel and Elaine tried to sell it.

An editor at Little, Brown wanted to publish it and took me to lunch, but she was overruled by higher-ups. No one else was interested in my great American taxicab novel.

I was becoming desperate again because I felt certain that I would be murdered some night while driving on NYC's mean streets. An average of four cabbies were murdered every month during that era.

Finally I decided to write whatever was necessary to get published and escape cabdriving. That's when the possibility of a dirty book occurred to me. Many well-known writers such as Henry Miller and Anais Nin among others had got their starts writing dirty books. Back then it was considered a completely honorable way to break into professional writing. I made a pact with myself. If I couldn't write and sell a dirty book, I'd give up writing and go back to PR if anyone would hire me.

My first step was to go to Times Square dirty book stores and look at actual dirty books, to see what was getting published. Many of the books were about sado-masochism which completely turned me off. I wasn't interested in whipping women and certainly didn't want them whipping me.

The classiest covers were from a publisher called

Midwood. I went home, called Midwood and was told that they'd send me their guidelines.

The guidelines soon arrived in the mail. They consisted of two mimeographed pages. Among the items was a warning not to write about children or animals. Included was a requirement that I should use actual crude pornographic words instead of nice scientific words like penis and vagina. That was the sum and substance of the guidelines that I recall.

What should I write about? I had to write about the kind of sex that turned me on most, because I couldn't write effective erotica about anything else.

What kind of sex turned me on the most? It depended upon whom I was with. Therefore, my female main character would have to be the kind of chick who turned me on most. She was a dream girl fantasy figure who became Patti, a perky, pretty, fun-loving blonde around 21 years old.

What would be the plot? I had read about honeymoon hotels in the Pocono Mountains of Pennsylvania, around 100 miles west of NYC, so used one of them as locale of a narrative consisting of consenting adults merrily having orgies and switching partners on their honeymoons in a Poconos honeymoon hotel. For drama, various participants become jealous, and some including Patti decide to leave their newly wedded spouses because they found better sex elsewhere.

To ramp up the action, a well-intentioned sex maniac chef flavors his dishes with aphrodisiacs!

But love always wins in the end because essentially my dirty book was a romantic novel about true love, believe it or not.

I was not married while writing this dirty book, nor did I have a girlfriend. Cabdriving and writing did not leave time for a social life which meant I was craving sexual relations. Which meant my erotic novel was infused with my own intense sexual desire.

I must be crazy to admit all this on paper, but my goal as a writer is to tell the truth no matter what and let chips fall where they may. I'm not going to stop now.

I was in a state of crazed sexual excitement while writing this novel, which transferred to pages I was typing. I soon realized that a pornographer probably understands his sexuality better than most people because a pornographer can read all his sexual obsessions in black and white on the printed page and become appalled by himself.

Finally I completed the novel, called it *Patti's Honeymoon* by Thomas Goona, and submitted it to Midwood. A few weeks later an editor called, said he loved it, found the story amusing, he'd publish it, and invited me to his office on Park Avenue South.

I don't remember his name. At our meeting he explained that Midwood was part of a publishing mini-conglomerate named Belmont-Tower that published other kinds of novels. He asked if I was interested in writing a Mafia novel. (That was during *The Godfather* craze.) Naturally I said yes.

He walked me down the hall and introduced me to Peter McCurtin, editor of action/adventure novels at Belmont-Tower, who himself had written many action/adventure novels, and resembled the TV star Arthur Godfrey. Peter asked me to write a novel in Belmont-Tower's *Sharpshooter* Mafia series, gave me two Mafia books of his to read, and that's how my career as an action/adventure writer began.

Midwood changed my dirty book title *Patti's Honeymoon* by Thomas Goona to *Private Sessions* by March

Hastings. The editor said that he wanted an androgynous name that would appeal to both men and women.

Recently I discovered that a real writer named Sally Singer, who wrote lesbian erotica, invented the pseudonym March Hastings for herself, which means Midwood ripped off her pseudonym for my novel.

In 2003 I left NYC to live in a Chicago suburb with one of my daughters, until I found a place nearby of my own. I didn't want her to ever see *Private Sessions* so threw out my first edition desk copy with original cover, an act which I now regret. I have been unable to find the original cover on the internet, only two other new covers. Evidently Midwood and its parent company Belmont-Tower reprinted my dirty book many times with different covers but never paid me royalties. Belmont-Tower went bankrupt a few years ago and Amazon bought the BT backlist, according to what I read.

I wrote a letter to Amazon inquiring about royalties and received a response stating that they had bought some books on the B-T backlist but not mine, so I'll never get those royalties.

I never wrote another hardcore XXX-rated erotic novel. I didn't want to go through that insane sexual fervor again. Once was interesting and fun but once was enough already.

And strangely enough, around 12 years after writing *Private Sessions* I became involved with a perky, pretty, fun-loving blonde in her twenties, the very incarnation of Patti, which proves yet again that dream girls can come true.

4

MY FIRST ACTION/ADVENTURE NOVEL

DURING THAT FIRST MEETING WITH PETER MCCURTIN, HE asked me to write a novel in their *Sharpshooter* series under the pseudonym Bruno Rossi, about an Italian male named Johnny Rocelli who calls himself Johnny Rock. His family had been killed by the Mafia and he seeks revenge by killing Mafia personnel. Peter explained that the *Sharpshooter* series was a rip-off of their similar *Marksman* series.

He gave me two of his novels as examples of requisite style, and also a *Marksman* novel for context. Describing Johnny Rock, Peter said, "He kills in cold hate."

I went home, studied Peter's novels and was impressed by his clean, fast-paced style reminiscent of Mickey Spillane, one of my all-time favorite writers. Somehow I needed to emulate that style.

I felt tremendous pressure about my first *Sharpshooter*. I needed to write a novel that Peter would accept, although I'd never written an action/adventure novel before. If I didn't please Peter, I'd need to get a regular job and give up my efforts to become a novelist.

It was another of my life's major crossroads. What would my first action/adventure novel be? I knew it had to start with an action scene to grab the reader's attention. Somehow I had to pull it off in grand style.

I found myself thinking about Little Italy where I actually had lived in a tiny roach-infested pad at 213 Mulberry Street for around a year approximately 1962, so I was familiar with the territory and aware that the first floor of my building, or perhaps it was the building next door, was ostensibly a social club but actually a Mafia hangout. Cadillacs with license plates from New Jersey and New York were parked at the curb and across the street. Well-dressed Italian guys examined me warily as I walked to work in the morning, dressed in one of my snazzy business suits, carrying my leather attache case.

I often wandered around Little Italy then and in subsequent years because it was an interesting area, like visiting Naples. I passionately loved Italian food and had a favorite inexpensive Italian restaurant on Broome Street, don't remember the name. I also regularly bought a pound of smoked mozzarella cheese made on site in a store called Alleva at 188 Grand Street. That pound of smoked mozzarella never lasted more than two hours.

I was not living in Little Italy in 1972 when Joey Gallo got shot multiple times gangland style at Umberto's Clam House at 132 Mulberry Street, a short distance from where I had lived. After the hit, I rode the subway downtown to Little Italy to see the restaurant which was scene of the crime. The hit was much in the news back then, no agreement to this day about who ordered and did the hit.

While wondering what opening scene to write for my *Sharpshooter*, the Joey Gallo hit came to mind. I decided that Johnny Rock would be dining in a clam house like

Umberto's, planning to kill two Mafia guys sitting nearby.

Elements in my memory combined with my vivid imagination to produce my first scene, a process which set the pattern for stories and characters for the rest of my literary career.

The narrative flowed easily from the first sentence. Somehow, miraculously, I was able to emulate Peter's style. I wrote *The Worst Way to Die* in about six weeks. Even more miraculously, I actually enjoyed writing it because, evidently, I had and still have a pulp fiction soul.

After completion I delivered the manuscript in person to Peter who called a few weeks later, said he liked it, and asked me to come to his office for a discussion about my next *Sharpshooter*.

I was elated after the phone conversation. Suddenly I was a real writer earning real money! I felt like I'd just hit a grand slam home run.

I went to the next meeting with Peter who began by critiquing my first *Sharpshooter*. He essentially said that I had made Johnny Rock too emotional, too worried about moral implications of his killings, too inclined to doubt himself. In other words, too much of me was in my version of Johnny Rock. Peter said that my Johnny's inner struggles would slow him down and make him too conspicuous, which would cause him to be killed. I had to calm down Johnny and make him more focused. Peter repeated his admonition, "He kills in cold hate."

I followed his advice, wrote two additional *Sharpshooters*, then Peter assigned me other books to write. Thus did my career as an action/adventure writer begin.

5

MY SECOND
ACTION/ADVENTURE NOVEL

I'VE NEVER FORGOTTEN *NIGHT OF THE ASSASSINS*, MY second action/adventure novel, because my editor Peter McCurtin called while I was writing it. He said: "The artist wants to put a helicopter on the cover, so write in a helicopter."

I asked: "Do you want it taking off, landing, or just flying around?"

"Have it flying around, with guys in it shooting at Johnny, and Johnny shooting back."

To my best recollection, I wrote the helicopter sequence into the same scene I was writing when Peter called. I will present the actual scene below but first should provide background so it will make sense.

Night of the Assassins was #5 in Leisure Books' *Sharpshooter* series by Bruno Rossi, starring Johnny Rocelli a/k/a Johnny Rock who is wreaking vengeance against the Mafia that murdered his family. *Night of the Assassins* was published in 1974.

Peter previously had told me to set the story in Miami which was fine with me because I had lived in

Miami Beach for around 10 months in 1953-54, and around one year in Miami itself beginning approximately 1966, so I was familiar with the terrain.

Setting the novel in Miami was the only instruction that Peter gave me in our initial discussion. That meant I'd need to invent the plot which wasn't difficult because it would be the usual *Sharpshooter* narrative about Johnny Rock slaughtering Mafia personnel, blood splattering in all directions, but I needed to add my own special brand of drama, suspense, intrigue, romance and all other necessary story elements, which I enjoyed figuring out and writing.

Regarding the scene that I was working on when Peter called, Johnny Rock is outdoors at night near a riverfront Mafia mansion and a boat. A load of cocaine is in crates near the boat. Johnny is holding a machine gun of the type called by the U.S. Army a grease gun and has just mowed down numerous Mafia personnel. Then he decides to leave. Below is the actual scene in the novel:

> Johnny decided to get moving fast, but thought he should destroy the drugs first. With his grease gun he opened fire at the crates. The wood and packing blasted apart, then white powder exploded all over the beach. Johnny fired until he thought he had demolished the load, but as he released his trigger, was surprised by the loud noise of an engine above.
>
> He looked up and saw a helicopter swooping down toward him out of the sky. There was one man in front piloting it, and at an open side door, another man crouched and aimed a rifle at Johnny. The rifle fired and sand erupted near Johnny's feet. Johnny dropped to one knee and fired up at the helicopter, but it kept circling.

After much back and forth firing Johnny finally shoots down the helicopter, it crashes in a fiery burst, and he makes good his escape. End of scene.

Many years later, while writing my semi-autobiographical novel *The Last Buffoon*, about an action/adventure writer based loosely on me, I reproduced my conversation with Peter and how it played out. It was just another incident in my crazy deadline-driven career as an action/adventure writer.

6

THE THRILL KILLERS

AFTER MY *SHARPSHOOTERS*, ALL MY SUBSEQUENT BELMONT-Tower books began with informal discussions with either Peter McCurtin or Milburn Smith at Belmont Tower's editorial offices at Park Avenue South and 33rd Street in midtown Manhattan. After I delivered a new completed manuscript to one or the other, I sat beside my editor's desk and received my next assignment.

The Thrill Killers followed this pattern. I sat beside Peter's desk, and he asked me to write a novel for one of their cop series, don't remember the name 40 years later because the name was changed as will be explained below. Peter either gave me one or more books in the series or just described it to me, I don't remember.

After the meeting I walked home to my pad on West 55th Street between 8th and 9th Avenues, wondering what the plot would be. There were so many possibilities.

Around that time, I'd read a true crime book about the sensational Leopold-Loeb murder case in Chicago during the 1920s. Two young college students at the

University of Chicago named Nathan Leopold and Richard Loeb decided they were Nietzsche-style supermen beyond good and evil, and plotted the perfect murder to prove their thesis. So they killed 14-year-old Bobby Franks but weren't as superior as they'd thought because soon afterwards they got busted and went to trial, defended by the legendary lawyer Clarence Darrow who argued not for their innocence, because evidence was overwhelming against them, but Darrow successfully saved them from the death penalty.

The Leopold-Loeb murder influenced the plot of *The Thrill Killers*. My detective's character profile followed the guidelines of what Peter told me in his office, a real badass cop obsessed with justice and couldn't care less about administrative procedures and laws that seemed more concerned with protecting criminals than catching, prosecuting and punishing them. The detective is not above administering the death penalty himself to murderers, often using their own methods against them.

After working on the novel for several days, I received a call from Peter. He said something like, "We're spinning off a new cop series about a detective named Joe Blaze. So change the detective's name to Joe Blaze and keep going."

I replied, "But his character and personality are based on (the name of the detective in the series I had been working on)."

Peter said, "Don't worry about that. Just change his name to Joe Blaze and keep going."

(I wrote a fictionalized version of this discussion with Peter into my semi-autobiographical novel about an action-adventure writer *The Last Buffoon* by Leonard Jordan, because it was one of the stranger experiences of my strange so-called literary career.)

I read *The Thrill Killers* recently for the first time in 40 years. I had forgotten it almost completely and as usual when reading one of my old books, it seemed to have been written by someone else.

At the risk of sounding immodest, I thought the book pretty good mainly because narrative tension held steady all the way through, and Detective Joe Blaze was a believable character, his anger about crime reflecting my own anger as resident of Manhattan during the high crime era before Rudy Giuliani became mayor, and Bill Bratton became commissioner of Police.

The novel presents a brutal view of the world which reflected what I read daily in New York newspapers and true crime novels. Murderers by definition don't care about laws or rules of civility. They have monstrous minds, and some are sadistic like the murderers in *The Thrill Killers*.

Wouldn't it be nice if we all loved each other or at least treated each other respectfully? But we don't; the human race never has, and this hardcore realistic viewpoint was the philosophical foundation for the novel.

New York City crime is increasing again according to news reports. Where is Joe Blaze now that we really need him again?

7

I WAS NELSON DEMILLE
(BRIEFLY)

ONE AFTERNOON IN 1973 I WAS SITTING IN THE PARK
Avenue South office of Peter McCurtin, my editor at
Belmont-Tower. I'd just delivered a manuscript and we
were discussing my next assignment.

Peter asked me to write a novel in a series called
Ryker created by one of BT's other writers Nelson
DeMille, whom I'd never heard of before. That was long
before Nelson DeMille became a best-selling author,
back when he was just another razzle-dazzle action/ad-
venture writer in the BT stable. Martin Cruz Smith also
was there at that time. I never met him either.

Peter said the deadline was coming due for Nelson's
Ryker novel, but Nelson couldn't write it because he was
busy with something else, which Peter didn't specify.

Peter didn't provide a plot or anything else. I needed
to invent plot, characters, etc., except for the character of
Ryker who was the basic badass NYPD detective. I'd
already written one badass cop novel for BT, the previously mentioned *The Thrill Killers* starring "Super Cop

Joe Blaze", so Peter knew I understood what was required.

That was around the time Patti Hearst got kidnapped by the Symbionese Liberation Army. It also was around the time some weathermen blew themselves to smithereens in a building not far from where I lived in west Greenwich Village.

Revolutionaries were much in the news back then, occasionally killing cops. Rebellion was in the air. Those current events became my fundamental plot elements, in addition to my own frustrations, anger and ongoing concerns about paying the rent.

I wrote *The Terrorists* in around six weeks which means it's not smooth as a novel written, re-written and polished a year or more. *The Terrorists* is rough and raw, I know, I know. I re-read it around a year ago and thought it quite good despite how rapidly it was written, but I'm hardly an objective critic of my novels. (It was published under the imprint of Leisure Books, one of BT's subsidiaries.)

Many years later, in the 1990s, I received a letter from Nick Ellison who identified himself as Nelson DeMille's literary agent. Nick essentially asked me to sign away my rights to *The Terrorists* and offered no payment or anything else.

The Terrorists didn't mean anything to me back then because I'd written it long ago and was busy with other projects. It never occurred to me that it might become a valuable property someday, although I should have known better because a writer never knows when he might hit the jackpot.

Blinded by my usual desperation, I hatched a really dumb plot. If I signed away my rights, perhaps Nick Ellison would agree to become my literary agent and make me a literary star like Nelson DeMille. I was working on a crime novel at the time that I hoped he'd sell for big bucks.

So I signed away my rights and asked Nick to represent the crime novel. He responded that he'd never been very successful with crime novels, and curtly turned me down.

In other words, I signed away rights to a novel for nothing. Zilch. Zero. Now I wonder how I could have made such a stupid decision. I become angry with myself whenever I think of it.

On my scale of values, Nick Ellison had a perfect right to ask me to sabotage myself. He was only representing his client's best interests, which was his job. Nobody forced me to sign anything. Nick Ellison is not to blame for anything. I was motivated by hope, dreams and the usual craziness of a marginally successful writer constantly worried about paying the rent. The blame is 100% mine because I'm an idiot occasionally.

My advice to all writers out there: **Don't ever sign away rights to anything you've written, no matter how desperate you might feel at the moment, because you'll regret it for the rest of your life!**

8

THE NOVEL I WROTE WITH THE GREAT PETER MCCURTIN

IN 1977, DURING A MEETING WITH PETER MCCURTIN, HE asked me to complete a novel that he began but couldn't finish. He'd written the first 30 pages or so, and I'd need to write the rest.

I walked home to my apartment in Hell's Kitchen and went to work. All basic decisions of plot, characters and locale already were in place, so I didn't need to invent anything. I just followed what Peter had written.

The Camp was about a military installation ostensibly for training U.S. soldiers but used by a secret cabal of U.S. Army officers to incarcerate hippies and other subversive dissidents. These officers were planning a military takeover of the U.S. government which they considered hopelessly corrupt.

Primary locales were in Maine where Peter had a home. I had visited Maine many times and in fact had hoped to settle there someday, so knew the landscape.

But I wasn't Peter McCurtin. I have my own weird imagination which I applied to Peter's 30 pages. The result was *The Camp*. My section reflects my attitudes at the time grafted on Peter's premise and attitudes. I haven't read *The Camp* for over 40 years, but my best recollection is that it was a very peculiar novel.

9

MY FIRST STANDALONE NOVEL

WAY BACK IN EARLY 1970S, AFTER WRITING SEVERAL
novels in series developed by Belmont-Tower, I decided
to make my own personal bid for literary fame and
fortune.

In order to accomplish those great goals, I'd need to
write a great standalone novel. What should I write
about?

As I looked over the bestseller literary scene, I felt
most attracted to spy novels by John Le Carré, Jack
Higgins, Robert Ludlum, Eric Ambler, Frederick
Forsyth, Alistair MacLean, Ken Follett and others of that
ilk. I especially liked John Le Carré's supreme skill with
character development.

So I started inventing my new spy novel that I hoped
would turn my whole life around. The leading man
David Brockman was based loosely on me as a CIA
agent. The leading lady Miralia Guzman was based
loosely on my first wife, a Cuban refugee. The plot was
based on important historical events of that era which I

28

won't describe in detail because I don't want to spoil anyone's reading experience.

Brockman gets out of prison on the first page. He had been busted in New York City while on a clandestine CIA mission involving photocopying documents in the Sutton Place apartment of a U.S. Congressman who allegedly had been passing secrets to a foreign power. The district attorney charged Brockman with burglary, and Brockman got eight years hard time.

Astonishingly, the CIA never bailed him out or extracted him from prison. He served his hard time seething with resentment against those who had betrayed and abandoned him. To quote from pages #1 and #2:

> No longer were there iron bars and stone walls between him and the rest of the world. He was a free man but only in the sense that he was not locked in a cell. He was not free to ignore those who had caused him go to prison and permitted him to languish there. The burglary had been an official CIA operation, or so they led him to believe.

Now he wants answers and will go to great lengths to get them. I called the novel *Betrayed*, delivered the completed version to my then literary agent Elaine Markson, who submitted it to various publishers.

Warner Paperback Library contracted to publish it. A young editor there, I think his name was Richard Fleischer, really liked it. I went to his office, and he praised my novel to high heavens. I thought I was on my way to the bestseller list and possibly a movie deal.

Warner changed the title to *Operation Perfidia*, and for the first time I could choose whatever author's name I wanted. After much thought I decided not to use my real name. The novel was controversial, and I thought someone might try to kill me, so decided on my first and middle names, Leonard Jordan.

Operation Perfidia was published in 1975. When I received my author's copies, I was disappointed with the cover. It showed a guy with oddly shaped body grimacing while holding an automatic rifle of strange manufacture, his trigger hand awkwardly bent, his trigger finger seemingly pulling the trigger down, his haircut atrocious. I considered the painting semi-amateurish, nothing like classy John Le Carré covers. Obviously Warner didn't spend much on the cover because evidently the Warner brass had low sales expectations. In fact, *Operation Perfidia* didn't sell very well so I returned to Belmont-Tower with my tail between my legs.

I never read the final published novel after I received my free copies. My last reading was of the original manuscript that I submitted to my literary agent. Then a few years ago I re-read *Operation Perfidia* for an article I wrote to accompany a review by Joe Kenney for his *GLORIOUS TRASH* blog.

I hadn't read the novel for around 40 years. When I cracked open my desk copy, it seemed new to me. I don't want to sound immodest, but I thought it really good except for a few awkward passages.

As I continued reading, the story came back to me. I couldn't wait for the ending because I remembered it as shocking, powerful and unexpected.

As the plot was building to my fabulous power ending – suddenly the story came to a screeching halt! I wondered if pages had fallen out. It didn't look that way. Evidently some editor at Warner had chopped off my great ending and never told me. At first, I couldn't imagine why he or she chopped it off. It wasn't a long book to begin with. But publishers often did whatever they wanted with writers like me who had no clout.

I guessed that Warner might have considered the novel as first of a possible series and wanted to keep the protagonist alive and viable as opposed to the dark John Le Carré-type ending I wrote for him. Or perhaps they didn't like my ending. And perhaps the weak cover and new truncated ending torpedoed any chances the novel might've had in the marketplace. Or perhaps those awkward passages did me in. Or perhaps the novel lacked qualities that make a best-seller, whatever those qualities are. Or perhaps the novel needed exotic foreign settings like John Le Carré books. Or perhaps I'm simply not John Le Carré and lack his Oxford education, career in British intelligence (MI5), and European sophistication. Or perhaps literary success is mostly a matter of luck.

So that's the backstory of *Operation Perfidia*. It's now available as an ebook and paperback by Len Levinson with the original power ending which I re-wrote from memory.

MY CAREER AS A CHINESE AUTHOR

THE YEAR OF THE BOAR BY LEE CHANG, PUBLISHED IN 1975, began with a phone call from an editor I knew at Belmont-Tower, don't remember his name. He said he was working for a new publishing house called Manor and asked if I would write for them. I said "sure", which was how a financially desperate freelance writer naturally would respond.

I lived on Christopher Street in Greenwich Village at the time, and either walked and/or rode subways to the meeting at Manor's office on Park Avenue South around East 32nd Street, in the same vicinity as Belmont-Tower.

In attendance at the meeting, in addition to the young man editor, was a young pretty lady editor whom I also had seen at Belmont-Tower. No one else was in the office which consisted of one medium-sized room with two desks, according to my memory 44 years later. I suspected that Manor was connected to Belmont-Tower in some way.

I don't remember details of the meeting but ended up writing two novels for Manor, *The Year Of The Boar* which was #6 in their *Mace* series by Lee Chang, and *Streets of Blood* in their *Bronson* series by Philip Rawls.

The Year Of The Boar really stimulated my imagination because I was interested in Eastern religions at that time, and had studied karate in the early 1960s under the great Okinawan master Ansei Ueshiro who worked out in class alongside students in his studio on West 14th Street in Manhattan. His speed, strength, agility and precision seemed almost supernatural. Inspired by him, I nailed a bamboo mat to a wall of my apartment and punched it to build up callouses on my knuckles, but my knuckles bled and no callouses ever happened.

In addition, I had studied Vedanta Hinduism plus Buddhism of the Theravada, Mahayana, Tibetan and Zen varieties, attended many lectures on these religions, read lots of books and actually practiced Hindu or Buddhist meditation exercises occasionally.

I also spent much time in NYC's vast Chinatown, largest Chinatown in America, which was spilling over into Little Italy and the Lower East Side. Often I explored out-of-the-way streets and alleys, hung out in Buddhist temples, ate in funky Chinese restaurants, and munched lotus seed buns as I wandered about. I wished I could move to Chinatown because I loved the exotic atmosphere, almost like being in Hong Kong.

I also watched a few Kung-Fu movies in Chinatown theaters, none of which had English subtitles but were fascinating anyway. The nearly 100% Chinese audiences seemed to enjoy them immensely. Those King Fu epics later influenced action scenes in *The Year Of The Boar* whose plot begins in Chinatown, and much of the action occurs there.

While writing *The Year Of The Boar*, I was having problems with my landlord because my apartment was rent-controlled and he wanted me to move out so he could jack up the rent. He refused to fix what was broken and threatened to have me beaten up if I complained to the Housing Authority. So he became the predominant villain of *The Year Of The Boar* and came to a very nasty end in the novel although continuing to harass me in real life.

All these experiences and semi-understood theologies became ingredients for *The Year Of The Boar*. As I skim through the novel today, I think the narrative was undermined by my annoying tendency to toss in sex scenes that seem casual and unmotivated, although a lot of sex seemed casual and unmotivated in the 1970s, which was the wild post-pill, pre-AIDS era. But I spent much of it sitting in a series of non-luxury apartments in Manhattan, writing action/adventure novels. To paraphrase Marcel Proust, it was life carried on by other means.

Below are excerpts from the review written about *Year Of The Boar* by Joe Kenney in his *Glorious Trash* blog. I should mention for sake of clarity that he refers to a writer named Joseph Rosenberger who wrote the first five novels in the Mace series and many other action/adventure novels.

I've been looking forward to this sixth volume of *Mace* for quite a while. Because my friends we're finally out of the weeds, i.e. the previous five volumes by Joseph Rosenberger, and as if in reward for enduring those five beatings we're graced with an installment by Len Levinson (using the same house name that Rosenberger did, 'Lee Chang'). So even though Len delivers a protagonist much different than his usual (at least when considering his other '70s novels), it goes without

saying that *The Year Of The Boar* is vastly more entertaining than any of Rosenberger's installments.

I know from Len himself that he never read those
previous five books; in fact as he most memorably
informed me once: 'I never heard of Joseph Rosenberger.' So for all intents and purposes this could be considered a standalone novel. And in many ways it is much
different from Len's other books of the decade, with a
straight-shooter protagonist wholly at odds with Len's
typical main characters from this era. In fact Victor
Mace is kind of boring, and makes one miss, for example, the neurotic Johnny Rock of Len's three *Sharpshooter* novels.

Overall, *The Year Of The Boar* was entertaining,
certainly when compared to Rosenberger's previous
five books, but at the same time I didn't enjoy it nearly
as much as Len's other books from this period. Not that
there's anything wrong with his prose or dialog, it's just
that it lacks that zany spark the others had. And mostly
I feel this is due to Mace himself, but again this isn't
Len's fault – he was hired to write a book about a kung-
fu master and that's how a kung-fu master is written. So
in that regard he certainly succeeded, but when you've
read say *Shark Fighter* (one of Len's later novels) you just
expect something more from the guy. I mean when a
cab driver who appears on maybe half a page total is
more memorable than the lead character, you know
something is up.

Joe raises an important issue. Kung Fu masters are
supposed to be steady, strong and imbued with wisdom.
They are not supposed to be neurotics and lunatics.
Unfortunately, as Joe points out, noble wise hero types
like Mace simply aren't as interesting as characters with

multiple neurotic complications. I should have made Mace more of a freak but never thought of it at the time, probably because my Manor editors might have disapproved and held up payment of the advance, which would have caused additional financial distress for a cash deficient freelance writer.

Another factor is that I tended to idolize Kung Fu, Zen and Karate masters, and other gurus and rishis, which is wrong because they're human beings with human weaknesses and flaws, and to treat them otherwise is to misrepresent their true natures and trivialize them, as Joe so accurately points out. Still, it was an interesting book to write, and it certainly felt good to kill my rotten landlord fictionally.

11

THE LIN CARTER FACTOR

LIN CARTER BECAME A BIG NAME IN THE SCI-FI AND sword and sorcery genres. He was a friend of mine and influenced me enormously. We met in 1962 when we were direct-mail advertising copywriters at Prentice-Hall publishing company in Englewood Cliffs, New Jersey.

Lin was approximately five years older than I and became one of my literary mentors. I was very impressed by his broad in-depth knowledge of literature. Back then we both wanted to become novelists. He gave me lists of books to read, was highly intelligent, erudite on many subjects, and dressed like a college professor with a bow tie.

At the time I met him, he lived with a rabbit named Watson in an apartment in the Bronx. I was living alone in Little Italy in Manhattan. We hung out together occasionally after work. Several times I met him at his favorite coffee house on MacDougal Street in Greenwich Village. A few times he invited me to screenings of old movie serials in apartments of his friends on Saturday afternoons in the East 70s of Manhattan.

One workday afternoon while riding a bus from New Jersey back to Manhattan, Lin told me that he believed in monarchies, not democracies. I wasn't sure if he meant it or was just putting me on.

He also told me that he had served in the Korean War, and jokingly referred to himself as "Red Bayonet Carter". He had been awarded a Purple Heart, so it wasn't all a joke.

I introduced him to a lady friend of mine named Claire with whom he became smitten and proposed marriage about a month later, but she turned him down. Then he met Noel Vreeland at Prentice-Hall and eventually they married. They seemed like a very good match, often tossing quips back and forth.

Around that time, he quit Prentice-Hall to write novels. His first was *The Wizard of Lemuria*. He gave me a copy which I still have. He also gave me a copy of his second: *Thongor of Lemuria*. I wasn't a sword and sorcery fan but thought these novels excellent.

Lin was a serious person most of the time. He definitely had gravitas. But he also liked to joke around occasionally. He did very good imitations of W.C. Fields. He could be very cruel verbally to people he didn't respect or like, but always was very genial with me.

Several times he invited me to dinner parties and other kinds of parties at the old wooden triple level home he and Noel shared in Hollis, Queens, which was full of bookcases. I have never seen so many books in a private home.

Lin and Noel were parents of approximately six huge vicious barking dogs who regularly freaked out and scared me half to death, as if they wanted to tear me limb from limb. A more interesting feature of the home was a skeleton hanging by his or her neck down the staircase. Lin and Noel were excellent hosts, their cuisine and liquor always first rate.

I also got married and saw less of Lin as I became involved with my family. I moved to Florida for a while, got divorced, finally returned to New York City, but never saw Lin again, although we talked on the phone every few years. I also became a novelist, but we were moving in different directions. At some point I became aware that he had become a big name in fantasy fiction.

I heard that he and Noel got divorced, and several years later, I think it was Noel who told me that he had mouth or face cancer. I spoke with him on the phone about two weeks before he died, when he was in a VA hospital. His voice sounded weak, and I thought he hadn't long for this world.

I'm now 85 years old and have met many distinctive individuals in my life. Lin certainly would rank in the top five. I considered him and still consider him a great man. He influenced my writing substantially through his dedication to literature, the wild quality of his imagination, his literary recommendations, my study of his clean writing style, and also perhaps by osmosis.

12

MY CAREER AS A SHARK FIGHTER

WAY BACK CIRCA 1976, MY EDITOR AT BELMONT-TOWER, the great Peter McCurtin, asked me to write a novel about a guy who signs a contract to fight a shark on closed circuit TV for a million bucks. That was pretty much all he said. I'd have to figure out the rest.

It was during the great *Jaws* craze when the media was full of articles and commentary on the movie and on shark lore. Peter wanted me to cash into that mass media fascination.

I never saw *Jaws* because it sounded like a water-logged horror story. I didn't and still don't like horror stories because their principal goal is to terrify me, and I don't like to be terrified. I have enough problems as it is.

I considered myself qualified to write an underwater shark story because I'd snorkeled in South Florida when I lived there on two different occasions, the first 1953-54, the second 1966-1967. I'd also dived several times with regulator and tank strapped to my back, so the undersea world was familiar and enjoyable for me. I also had watched many undersea TV programs by Jacques-

Yves Cousteau. I even read his book *The Silent World*. So all things considered, I felt enthusiastic and well-prepared to write *Shark Fighter*.

I departed Peter's office, went home and dived into *Shark Fighter*. My first creative decision was to up the ante over Peter's suggestion. Instead of one man fighting one shark for one million dollars, I wrote one man fighting two sharks simultaneously for two million dollars in a swimming pool on closed circuit TV.

Shark Fighter was published in 1977. I forgot it as years passed. Then in 2014 Joe Kenney asked me to write an essay to accompany his review of *Shark Fighter* for his *Glorious Trash* blog. I didn't remember characters and plot details so sat down and actually read my own novel for the first time in 37 years.

To my astonishment, I couldn't believe it was so interesting. In fact, it was so great, it read as if written by a very fine writer. I couldn't put it down. All my various obsessions and preoccupations of that era are in the novel. I'd often fantasized about living on a boat in the Caribbean, and one of my highest career goals was to become a full-time beachcomber. Naturally I'd always wanted a beautiful *Vogue*-type model to fall madly and hopelessly in love with me, as happened to Sam Taggart, protagonist of the novel.

Shark Fighter evidently was wish fulfillment expressed in the form of a novel. While reading it, I couldn't help noticing how smoothly and quickly the plot moved along. The reader cannot guess what will happen next, perhaps because the author didn't know either. The characters all had numerous neurotic compulsions and seemed like real believable people.

The island of Makura where the story takes place was based partially on Haiti under the dictator Papa Doc

Duvalier, and partially on the Dominican Republic under the dictator Rafael Trujillo, and partially on a trip I once took to Nassau in the Bahamas. *Shark Fighter* even has a fairly happy ending, unlike many of my novels.

As usual a few typographical errors either were overlooked or inserted by Belmont-Tower copy editors. The big shark fight at the end had a sentence that didn't know left hand from right hand which was confusing. Some sentences contained too many words. Perhaps the Belmont-Tower copy editor inserted them for grammatical correctness, or perhaps the culprit was me.

I might be prejudiced but *Shark Fighter* doesn't come across as simple-minded trashy fiction. It's more of an adventure melodrama with echoes of Joseph Conrad, Graham Greene, William Somerset Maugham and Groucho Marx, in my admittedly biased opinion. What a great movie it would make. I'm very proud of this novel, considering I wrote it in around six weeks. I'm grateful to Joe for returning it to my attention.

Below are some excerpts from Joe's review:

I'm about to rave about *Shark Fighter* – I loved it, and it was one of my favorite novels yet by Len.

To be sure, this novel has absolutely no pretensions. It's just a straight-up pulp tale about an ex-Navy frogman named Sam Taggart who accepts an offer to fight two sharks on live television for two million dollars. But man, the novel's a lot of fun, and this lack of pretense just adds to the charm. Taggart is part of the reason; like most every other Levinson protagonist, [he] is a no-nonsense guy who is focused on two primary things: women and money. Having served his time in 'Nam, he now enjoys life as a self-described "beach bum" on the fictional Caribbean island of Makura, where he hunts sharks for a living.

I almost wished I could book my next vacation in the Republic of Makura, which we are informed lies midway between Cuba and the Bahamas and measures 80 miles long and 20 miles wide. Here Taggart lives basically an idyllic life as he voyages around on his motorboat, smokes copious amounts of island-grown "ganja," and bangs whatever female he can talk into bed. He's chosen to make his living in a dangerous profession, hunting sharks and selling them to the chefs of the island's many five-star hotels. Taggart doesn't even make much on the deal, and acknowledges to himself that he basically has a death wish. He just likes to risk his life killing sharks.

I don't know, maybe *Shark Fighter* is like the trash fiction equivalent of *The Old Man and the Sea* [by Ernest Hemingway]. Or maybe not. At any rate, I enjoyed the hell out of it, and regret that it's not more easily available – though with some persistence you should be able to turn up an eventual copy.

Now back to me, Lenny. It gives me great pleasure to report that Shark Fighter is readily available right now, having been republished under my real name as paperbacks and ebooks. I fixed all typographical, grammatical, and other errors that I found in the original print edition, plus that awful left hand – right hand confusion.

Perhaps I was a better writer than I and many others thought at the time. Perhaps someone should nominate me for a Nobel Prize, or the National Book Award, or at least a MacArthur Award.

13

MY GREAT AMERICAN SALOON
NOVEL

I WROTE *THE BAR STUDS* BECAUSE I ENJOYED GOING TO bars when I lived in NYC and felt inspired to write about them.

I was drawn to bars not because I liked to drink, but because that's where the action was, where I could meet women and many other interesting people who were great conversationalists and storytellers.

During my 42 years in New York City, I visited numerous different species of bars such as Greenwich Village hangouts, East Side singles bars, Bowery dives, the Oak Room at the Plaza, gay men's bars in the Village, even one jaunt to a lesbian bar called The Duchess near Sheridan Square in the Village, where I felt distinctly unwelcome but really should not have been there because people have a right to privacy without a curious writer gawking at them.

I especially enjoyed a Village bar called Bradley's that featured live jazz. I'd give almost anything for another musical evening at Bradley's, but Bradley now is dead, and the bar no longer exists as far as I know (I no longer reside in NYC.).

I also especially enjoyed a joint called the Buffalo Roadhouse on 7th Avenue south of Sheridan Square, popular with wannabe actresses, models, dancers and nurses from nearby St. Vincent Hospital.

I conceived my bartender novel as "the varieties of bar experience", based on all the different New York bars I went to, and different people I met in bars, and situations I observed. It became a very ambitious novel with many plots and subplots. I was trying for the Great American Saloon Novel and hoped to be rewarded accordingly with wealth and fame.

I didn't need to invent what it was like to be a bartender because I had worked as one at a few joints in Lansing, Michigan when I was a student at Michigan State University. So I knew what it was like on the other side of the bar, rushing back and forth on the floor-boards, mixing, pouring, collecting money, making change, becoming embroiled in conversations and learning that inebriated people often spill their guts to bartenders, while certain women, after a few drinks, might flirt with the bartender who was not averse to flirting back. And occasionally a drunk wanted to fight the bartender, which required diplomatic skills of the highest order.

I began writing my Great American Saloon Novel around 1974. My working title was *The Bartenders* which told the stories of six bartenders, some of whom knew each other. For example, Adrian and Johnny worked in a Village bar similar to a combination of Bradley's and the Buffalo Roadhouse; Leo in an East Side singles bar similar to Maxwell's Plum; Teddy in a gay bar similar to

Ty's on the ground floor of the apartment building where I lived on Christopher Street in Greenwich Village; Jake was a funky Bowery bartender; and elegant gray-haired Houlihan mixed dry martinis and other libations for the upscale crowd in the Oak Room at the Plaza.

Actually the novel was about much more than bar life. Like all my novels, it also was about love, hate, violence, anger, envy, greed, frustration, and the pornography of everyday life, not to mention popular drugs of that era, plus the presence of Cosa Nostra in NYC night life.

The final result came to around 90,000 words. My then literary agent Elaine Markson sold publication rights to Fawcett, who changed the title to *The Bar Studs*, and produced what I considered a great cover. My Fawcett editor Harvey Gardner always referred to the novel as *The Bar Stools*.

Harvey asked me to add a new ending because he thought I had not satisfactorily resolved issues that I raised. Did I argue with him and insist on my artistic integrity and vision? Of course not. I wrote the new ending because perhaps he was right, and I dared not jeopardize the advance which I needed to pay the rent.

The Bar Studs was published in 1976 under my pseudonym Leonard Jordan, and became my best-selling novel, around 95,000 copies. I thought I finally was on my way to wealth, fame, and regular guest stints on *The Johnny Carson Show*, but never reached those august numbers again.

Regardless of failed ambitions, *The Bar Studs* was a great ride for me. I love that book and always will. It's about a New York City that's gone forever but never forgotten by people who were there.

Of course, the novel includes inevitable examples

here and there of my occasional clumsy writing and egregious bad taste, but I was a sleazy character myself in those days and couldn't help myself. Now I'm trying to be a dignified elderly gentleman, without much success I'm sorry to say.

Joe Kenney wrote a review of *The Bar Studs* for his *Glorious Trash* blog, published on January 20, 2014. In one of his paragraphs, he said:

> If like me you're fascinated by the sleazy '70s, then you'll definitely dig **The Bar Studs**, as Len peppers the novel with all kinds of period details. And speaking of sleaze he also serves up lots of graphic sex scenes, leaving little to the imagination as Johnny Mash gets his rocks off (while holding a knife to the poor lady's throat!) or as Adrian has sex in his loft apartment above the bar with Julie. Drug use is also rampant, with characters snorting coke and smoking dope with abandon – and, best of all, with none of the "moral implications" that would be forced upon such scenes in today's world. These people just want to get stoned and fuck, and what's wrong with that?"

What indeed?

The Bar Studs has been republished in paperback and as an ebook under my real name.

14

MY GREAT AMERICAN PRESS
AGENT NOVEL

THROUGHOUT MY SO-CALLED LITERARY CAREER, MY
primary goal was to write one novel per year and earn
lots of dough, instead of writing around six novels per
year and living in borderline financial disaster accompanied by mental exhaustion at the end of each day.

After The Bar Studs I decided to really go for the gold
in the form of a best-selling Harold Robbins-type show
biz novel based on my ten years as press agent in the
entertainment industry in New York City from around
1962 to 1971.

I'd worked for Paramount Pictures, 20th Century-
Fox, and as mentioned previously, a show biz PR agency
named Solters and Sabinson which had clients like
Frank Sinatra, Barbra Streisand, Bob Hope, Dolly
Parton, Michael Jackson, Ringling Brothers and Barnum
& Bailey Circus, the Playboy organization, the Beatles,
Rolling Stones, and many other big names in addition to
many movies and Broadway shows.

This experience afforded me a unique view of show
biz behind-the-scenes, where vanity, unreasonable

demands, temper tantrums, ruthless ambition, and other insane behavior reigned supreme, in contrast to glossed over crap in the media.

But it wasn't all insane. I also met many decent, talented, rational people during my press agent years.

Fortunately or unfortunately, I wasn't Harold Robbins by any stretch of the imagination. He and I experienced different facets of the biz, he an executive accountant who occasionally attended meetings, I a press agent dealing with performers, the media, and my various not-always-nice bosses.

I also have peculiar tendencies toward comedy and satire in contrast to Robbins who wrote straight up prose. However, I don't intend to put him down. I read his novel *The Dream Merchants* when I was a teenager and thought it magnificent. It inspired me to work in the film industry someday, and that's where I ended up after graduating Michigan State University class of 1961.

The plot of *Hype!* centers around a hustling unscrupulous press agent named Mike Brown based loosely on me. His boss, Larry Walters, was based loosely on my boss Lee Solters, one of the great legendary press agents of all time. If you don't believe me, check Wikipedia. Other characters also were based loosely on real people, some very famous.

All my churning emotions, feelings and observations about show biz were poured into this morally atrocious novel. I held nothing back from my up close and personal experiences in the sordid subterranean depths of show biz.

I called the novel *The Shucksters* which I considered an absolutely brilliant title. After completing and editing the text, I submitted it to my then literary agent, the very wonderful Elaine Markson. Eventually she sold it to

Fawcett, same publisher of *The Bar Studs*. Fawcett changed the title to *Hype!*. My same editor Harvey Gardner explained that most Americans probably wouldn't know what a "shuckster" was. It was published in 1977 under my pseudonym Leonard Jordan, same as *The Bar Studs*.

I wasn't happy with the murky cover that didn't stand out against other novels in bookstores. The graphic artist used a strange typeface that made Hype! look like *Hypel*. Talks with Harvey left me with the impression that some Fawcett execs hadn't been very enthusiastic about the novel, because they considered it too controversial and vulgar. Harvey had managed to convince them that readers of *The Bar Studs* probably would also buy *Hype!*.

Harvey was wrong. *Hype!* became a big flop. I think it only sold around 27,000 copies, very little for a mass market paperback. It was one of the greatest professional disappointments of my life, but even greater professional disappointments were to come.

In 2014 Joe Kenny asked me to write something to accompany his review of *Hype!* on his *Glorious Trash* blog. So I read the novel for the first time since completing the manuscript forty years earlier circa 1974.

To my immense satisfaction I thought it one of the great unacknowledged show biz novels of all time. I admit it's as sleazy as the subject itself and also kind of vicious, definitely not a conventional lurid novel about kinky upper-class people as written by Harold Robbins or Jackie Collins. My no-bullshit scudsy approach probably harmed its prospects in the marketplace, but I could only write the truth as I had seen it.

What was the truth? Evidently I was an angry man when I wrote this novel, making critical uncomplimentary observations about all sorts of people, institutions and political movements, which probably explains why some Fawcett execs disapproved of *Hype!*. Such a novel never could be published in today's politically-correct climate.

Here are some comments from Joe Kenney's review of *Hype!* which was posted on 5/20/2014.

> *Hype!* tells the tale of a New York City Public Relations firm, its wacky clients and its even wackier employees. [It] really isn't much like Harold Robbins – the characters are too three-dimensional for that, and you can tell that Len, unlike Robbins, is actually having fun writing – but it *is* a lot like *The Bar Studs*, in that it's about a fairly large cast of eclectic characters in funky '70s NYC.
>
> *Hype!*, rather than telling a single plot, instead comes off like a series of misadventures these various characters experience. For Mike it's hustling one person or business after another, with little time for a private life – but then, Mike just combines the two. While on the job he snorts tons of cocaine, smokes dope, and even manages to have sex with a Stag Club "Doe" in the Stag Club itself, snorting some coke with the gal and then doing her up against the wall. Throughout the novel he'll randomly head on over to the apartment of his drug dealer, Perce Washington, a black guy who has a constant party going on (that is until he smokes some Nepalese hash, which sends Perce into a three-day meditative trip in which he questions reality).

The novel's Stag Club was based on the New York Playboy Club on 59th Street between 5th Avenue and Madison Avenue, one of my clients when I was a press agent at Solters and Sabinson. Stag Club Does were my literary version of Playboy Club Bunnies.

Whatever happened to all those gorgeous Bunnies of yesteryear? They're probably all grandmas now, as I'm a grandpa, but more importantly: whatever happened to *Hype!*? Thankfully it has been republished in paperback and as ebooks under my real name Len Levinson, for anyone who dares to dive into the tawdry nether regions of glitzy show biz.

15

JOHN LENNON AND ME

PERHAPS I SHOULD MENTION THE HIGHLIGHT OF MY PRESS agent career, which was meeting and working with John Lennon.

My encounter with him began one morning during winter of 1969-1970, at the height of the Vietnam War. I was a 34-year-old press agent sitting at my desk at Solters and Sabinson, a show biz PR agency on West 45th Street between 5th and 6th Avenues near Times Square.

I was writing a press release when my boss Sheldon Roskin suddenly appeared before my desk and announced he and I were leaving for Toronto in a few hours, to manage publicity for John's and Yoko's latest Peace-In. Sheldon said: "Go home and pack."

What was our connection with John Lennon? One of our most important clients was Allen Klein, a talent agent and manager whose most famous client was John Lennon.

A chauffeured limousine was waiting at the curb of the office building. I was driven home to my East Village pad, packed, returned to the office, picked up Sheldon, we were driven to La Guardia airport, flew to Toronto, arrived around 5pm, checked into the Hilton, and cabbed immediately to a university auditorium.

Inside was tremendous hullabaloo. At the podium, someone delivered an emotional antiwar speech. Sheldon and I attempted to acquaint ourselves with reporters and photographers during simmering chaos.

Three or four additional antiwar speeches were made, then John was introduced. Wild applause accompanied him as he approached the podium. I'd never seen him in person before. Approximately 5 feet 7 inches, slim, long-haired, long-bearded, wearing loose-fitting plain sweater and slacks in earth tones, he projected no glitz, didn't wave to the audience like a star, and if I didn't know better, I'd guess an English major or wannabe poet.

Standing at the podium, gazing levelly at the audience, not reading from a prepared statement, he spoke simply and sincerely, not like a stand-up comic or politician. I didn't have a tape recorder or write what he said in a notebook, but essentially, he implored the world to give peace a chance, like his song. His talk lasted around fifteen minutes and received tremendous applause.

Afterwards, Sheldon and I rode in a limousine to the outskirts of Toronto, finally stopping at a three-story mansion in an affluent suburb where everyone owned several acres, massive lawns, stands of trees, and country chic.

The mansion was home to American rockabilly star Rockin' Ronnie Hawkins and his family. John, Yoko and their entourage were living and hanging out at Ronnie's during their Toronto peace campaign.

Sheldon and I entered through the kitchen, and

Sheldon kept truckin' to the next room, a large combination dining/living area, where a sizable schmooze-type party was underway. Sheldon needed to report to John, and I should accompany him like a faithful underling, but got distracted by the male and female cooks working before a restaurant-style range.

I'd seen both before: they were husband and wife cooks at The Cauldron, arguably the East Village's most popular macrobiotic restaurant, Sixth Street between Second and First Avenues.

I said: "Hey – I know you people! I eat in your restaurant two-three times a week."

We shook hands and fell into our favorite subject: "the diet". In that long ago era, many thoroughly progressive and quite hip individuals were subsisting on the macrobiotic diet, popularized in the West by Georges Ohsawa, based on Zen Buddhist principles, believed to prevent or cure all physical and mental ills. The diet consisted mainly of brown rice, beans, certain vegetables, seaweed, sesame sauce, miso, tahini, sea salt and a bit of fish now and then, but don't overdo it. I'd been on the diet around three months and expected my breakthrough to total enlightenment any moment.

The cooks explained that John had hired them to fly to Toronto and cook for him, Yoko and the entourage. As we continued discussing "the diet", John himself wandered into the kitchen. Evidently he'd been near the door, heard us talking and wanted to participate.

Again, I didn't have a tape recorder and didn't write notes. To the best of my recollection, face-to-face, John came across as amiable, bright and very knowledgeable about "the diet". Neither over-confident or diffident, seemingly at ease in his skin, a regular guy with odd

Liverpool accent, John in the flesh was far different from his media image as temperamental genius.

The cooks needed to return to dinner prep, so John and I proceeded to the dining/living area, where other people approached him, and we became separated. Like a good press agent, I worked the room, met many journalists and antiwar activists, including a lanky, white-haired, antiwar rabbi and his wraithlike, white-haired wife who were minor celebrities recently returned from Hanoi after meeting Ho Chi Minh. The rabbi showed me a cane that good Uncle Ho had given him. He seemed quite proud of meeting Uncle Ho, who at that moment was busily killing as many American soldiers and Marines as possible.

I schmoozed around the gathering, bumped into John again and we resumed discussing "the diet". Standing nearby, the rabbi's wife interrupted: "Don't believe him, John. He's probably not really on the diet."

I couldn't imagine how to respond, after being insulted flagrantly by a total stranger – in front of a major client no less – and she the Rebbetzin no less!

Christians probably are unaware of the majestic figure of the rebbetzin in Jewish life and literature. Usually the rebbetzin managed her community's day-to-day practical affairs, while the rebbe studied Torah, taught classes, prayed, and had visions.

As a Jew, I felt overawed by this ebbetzin. How could I prove that I really was on "the diet"? I stared at her in disbelief, and she returned my stare triumphantly, as if seeing right through me, knowing I was a cheap con artist, and she thoroughly justified in exposing me.

Perhaps she worried about me gaining undue influence over John, since press agents generally were considered dishonest, saying anything necessary to ingratiate ourselves with clients and the press. Or she considered me a rival to be knocked out with one punch.

John appeared amused by this interaction. Smiling broadly, he slapped me on the shoulder. "Oh – I know he's on the diet."

Because he'd heard me rapping with his macrobiotic cooks – he knew I was legit. He could've kept quiet, not getting involved, but instead supported me, a noble gesture I thought. The rebbetzin looked crushed, which she thoroughly deserved.

Next morning, Sheldon and I returned to the suburban castle, my first assignment to sit alone in a den-type room, phoning journalists and disk jockeys across North America, setting up phone interviews with John, not strenuous effort because journalists and disk jockeys would sell their grandmothers into slavery for an opportunity to speak with John Lennon directly.

While dialing a disk jockey from some major market, I was surprised by John walking in, carrying an acoustic guitar. He sat on a nearby sofa and proceeded to strum or pick experimentally, the identical John Lennon who'd performed before 80,000 screaming fans at Shea Stadium in Queens, and now his audience consisted of one person – *moi*.

It was surreal. There sat one of the most famous human beings on the planet. But he looked like an ordinary person. It didn't make sense. I noticed John becoming uncomfortable, perhaps because I ogled him like a rabid fan. How could I make phone calls while he performed? Without a word, he arose and calmly left the room.

What did he have? Was it the aura of incredible fame? If I saw him plunking a guitar in a corner of an East

Village tenement party, another bearded face in the smoky crowd, would I be so moved?

I think so. Because he projected that peculiar attribute called charisma. What is charisma? Perhaps some kind of magic communicated by accomplished artists – in contrast to plunkers.

The Beatles were not your average white band. An original artistic vision propelled them to international fame. What is fame? Is it baloney? John couldn't even walk around downtown Toronto without besiegement by crazed fans, so hid in a mansion at the edge of town. Perhaps fame really is the booby prize.

John and Yoko spent most of every day alone together in their wing of the massive structure. Perhaps they wrote songs or poetry, sketched, engaged in philosophical or spiritual conversations, or listened to music. In Albert Goldman's biography of John, he and Yoko were retailed as heroin addicts, but they never nodded out or appeared befuddled in my presence.

Yoko came across as a loyal, quiet, alert wife, although the media spun her as the dragon lady. She and John entered rooms hand in hand, appearing deeply connected.

One afternoon, wandering around the top floor of the massive structure, looking for Sheldon, and getting lost, I opened a door and found a small room with approximately six young dudes sitting on the floor, passing a pipe and listening to a rock and roll tape I'd never heard before, the pungent fragrance of hashish in the air. I apologized for intruding, and they invited me to join them. Their hashish was quite potent. I got stoned out of my mind.

They informed me that the music was the new "Big Pink" album soon to be released, performed by a group called "The Band", which was Ronnie Hawkins's usual touring and recording band. Those same musicians also backed Bob Dylan on occasion. Someone put away the pipe, someone else opened a window, and we listened to "Big Pink" for what seemed several hours, but actually around 10 minutes.

Suddenly knuckles rapped the door; a member of the entourage opened up. In walked my boss Sheldon, who glanced at me sternly. "What the hell are you doing?"

"Just taking a rest."

"You're not being paid to rest. Don't ever hide from me this way again. Come with me – I want you to handle an interview."

In a living room on the ground floor, Sheldon introduced me to Howard Smith, thirty-something reporter for NYC's influential "Village Voice", plus Howard's tall, slender, blonde, twenty-something female assistant.

Sheldon departed. Howard fiddled with recording equipment; his assistant set up photo lights. Both appeared deeply serious, as if careers depended on the interview. My functions would be: (1) help resolve possible difficulties, and (2) take notes for column items.

John arrived, shook hands with Howard and his assistant, nodded to me, and sat. The interview commenced and turned adversarial quickly, although fairly cordial on the surface. For example, Howard asked John to comment on the contention in some quarters that the Beatles really were nothing special, but had been "made" by Brian Epstein, Derek Taylor, George Martin and various other movers and shakers.

John replied emphatically: "They didn't make us – we made them!"

Egomania? Nowadays virtually all rock historians agree that John, Paul, George and Ringo revolutionized rock and roll, admittedly with a little help from their friends.

While sitting in that interview, I understood how John's reputation for being temperamental and difficult had got started. Reporters asked him insulting questions and he came back at them. He didn't tolerate disrespect. So they called him temperamental and difficult because reporters are always right, at least in their articles.

Many years later, I read the bio of John by Albert Goldman. The interview with Howard Smith was mentioned. Goldman indicated that the interview had been amiable, which evidently is what Smith had told him. Not mentioned was other people in the room, Smith's girlfriend and the press agent Len Levinson who heard everything and knew the truth. The Goldman book reinforced what I already knew, that journalists and biographers do not always report the truth.

Maybe I'm way over the top with the Beatles. When they first burst onto the scene, I'd considered them mostly hype. Then I listened to the just-released "Revolver" vinyl album at a friend's apartment during summer of 1966. In the terminology of the day – it blew my mind. Totally. Because it sounded completely new, even thrilling, not a series of rock and roll songs but a symphony of human experience from sorrow to glory to the Tibetan Book of the Dead. Their next release "Sergeant Pepper" explored an entirely different dimension of poetry and magic. Sometimes I considered John an avatar of art.

No one would laugh harder at such a suggestion than John himself. Based on my first-hand observations, he didn't appear dazzled by fame in the least, probably considering it a torrent of mixed blessings suddenly dumping upon him through the fickle plumbing of fate.

After three nights in Toronto, Sheldon and I returned to our offices in NYC. But I never forgot my encounter with John Lennon. In retrospect, it seems the pinnacle of my press agent career, except possibly for a few days with Sophia Loren, who also was of heavenly origin, or a few days with Charleton Heston, who in real life was none other than Moses, or speaking briefly with the absolutely stunning Julie Andrews at the world premiere of "The Sound of Music", or standing around ten feet from Frank Sinatra at the world premiere of "Von Ryan's Express", or meeting twenty-something Raquel Welch at JFK, and escorting her in a chauffeured limo to a hotel no longer extant on 5th Avenue and 59th Street, first trip of her life to NYC, for the world premiere of "Fantastic Voyage" –plus my association with other celebrities of the soaring sixties.

In early 1971 I resigned PR to take a fling at becoming a novelist. Around six months later, banging away on my typewriter, I received a call from Sheldon. He'd been speaking with John, who asked: "How's my macrobiotic press agent?"

Awhile later, strolling on 8th Street in west Greenwich Village, I happened to glance through a jewelry store window, and spotted John and Yoko standing at the counter, examining trinkets. My first impulse was to walk inside, slap John on the back, and say: "How're ya doin', John? It's me –your former macrobiotic press agent."

But hangers-on and glad-handers irritate celebrities. So I kept on walking.

On December 8, 1980, I absent-mindedly turned on my television. An emergency newscast reported that John Lennon had just been shot in front of the Dakota apartment building where he lived on Central Park West and 72nd Street, only 17 blocks uptown from my pad on West 55th. He died in the Roosevelt Hospital emergency room, three blocks away. Coincidentally, I'd been a patient in that very emergency room, perhaps in the very cubicle where John passed on.

The Age of Aquarius ended for me when John Lennon was gunned down at the entrance to the Dakota. Evidently the hippie philosophy of peace, love, mind-altering chemicals, and rock and roll hadn't eradicated evil as we'd all hoped. Mentally-disturbed characters still walked the face of the earth, and some yearned to become celebrities, although possessing zilch talent.

It's not that difficult to become a celebrity. All you need do is murder a celebrity. Guaranteed your face will be on the front page of every newspaper next day and telecast around the globe as you climb the steps of the courthouse. You can wave to the crowd like a real star. You might even get a book contract!

Sometimes I felt partially responsible for the murder of John Lennon. As former press agent, I'd helped manipulate gears and levers of celebrity, creating illusions vastly different from reality, perhaps influencing certain psychotics adversely.

But violent individuals have walked this planet long before press agents existed. The decision to kill seems to come primarily from within, if you believe in free will. But insane people by definition don't have normal mental processes. Did unbalanced brain chemicals induced by organic dysfunction, or psychological trauma – kill John Lennon?

There's nothing inherently wrong with celebrity. Charismatic performers cannot avoid fame, for better or worse. That's why they need press agents. And bodyguards.

John's assassination taught me something else that I already knew but needed reminding. Evil won't disappear unless the human race also disappears. The devil doesn't walk around with horns, red suit, pointy tail and pitchfork. Instead, he's another face in the crowd, twisted inwardly by envy, hatred and fear.

John's murder didn't undermine my faith in the essential decency of most people. And I still enjoy listening to original Beatles albums on cd. I gave a new "Sergeant Pepper" cd to my grandchildren Rachel and David, when they were six and four years old. They loved it. So John lives on.

IN THE PULP FICTION TRENCHES

16

MY LITERARY CANADIAN
ADVENTURE

I LIVED ALONE IN A RACKETY OLD LOG CABIN IN A REMOTE wilderness region of New Brunswick, Canada from approximately 1974-1977.

The cabin had no electricity, plumbing or other modern conveniences. The dirt road to the cabin was not plowed during long frigid winters.

Why was I living in extreme isolated austerity? I wanted to be alone without distractions so I could concentrate on writing great best-selling novels that would elevate me out of the pulp fiction bump and grind. I also wanted to reduce my expenses drastically for the same reason. I'd written around 15 or 20 pulp fiction novels by that time.

My car was parked in the backyard of my landlord's home located on a plowed dirt road about a half-mile south of the cabin. Every few weeks I shopped for food and other supplies in the provincial capital of Fredericton approximately 52 miles to the south, then drove back to my landlord's home, strapped on snowshoes and dragged supplies on a toboggan over snow from my car to the cabin.

My landlord Ted Somerville was a lumberjack who lived in an old wood house with his family and electricity but no indoor plumbing. We were the only ones on his 500 wooded acres. His brother Gilbert and family lived in a different house farther down the dirt road.

A married couple who also were writers and friends of mine from New York City, William Kotzwinkle and Elizabeth Gundy, lived with electricity and plumbing on a plowed dirt road about three miles to the south. They, my landlord, his brother and their families comprised my entire neighborhood. No one lived north of me for many miles.

My water came from a spring brook approximately 60 yards down a hill from the cabin. Every day I filled a blue plastic barrel and carried it from the spring up the hill to the cabin. In deep winter I hatcheted through ice sometimes one inch thick or more.

After snowstorms I found little piles of snow on surfaces inside the cabin. Weatherproof it definitely was not. Neither was it mouse proof. Naturally there was no shower stall. Every Sunday I heated buckets of water on a wood stove, then bathed in a big aluminum tub. The whole messy process took several hours, water splashing on furniture and the floor.

About 30 yards behind the cabin slouched a weather-beaten superannuated wooden outhouse occupied occasionally by a porcupine who gnawed on the toilet seat and surrounding wood because urine salt was his addiction. Once I wielded a branch to pull and push him out so I could use the outhouse myself, trying not to injure him because he was not a bad guy intrinsically. He just needed his urine salt fix. It was quite a struggle because he was very stubborn, but finally I won. An outhouse in single digit temperatures was unforgettably horrible but somehow, I survived.

Often I saw bear manure while hiking during warmer weather. I also saw live deer, moose and eagles, among other critters. Doubtlessly wolves roamed the area but for some strange reason I wasn't afraid. Now I think that I should have been.

My diet consisted mostly of dry cereal, powdered milk, cheese, whole wheat bread, peanut butter, jam, and canned beans heated on the stove. My entertainment consisted of books or my battery-powered shortwave radio, which wasn't exactly Broadway or Lincoln Center. After sundown I read by the light of an Aladdin kerosene lamp.

I wrote three novels on my Underwood manual typewriter during the three years that I lived in the cabin. Two were published:

1. *The Bar Studs* by Leonard Jordan, Fawcett 1976, mentioned above.
2. *Hype!* by Leonard Jordan, Fawcett 1977, also mentioned above.

The third novel *The Bandit and the Ballerina* never was published. I never even submitted it to my literary agent. The novel became a disaster probably because I had no in-depth, behind-the-scenes knowledge of the ballet world, therefore could not write about it effectively despite having read many books on the subject, having met actual ballerinas socially, and having enjoyed many live ballet performances at Lincoln Center, City Center and other venues when I lived in NYC. Admiration of beautiful, graceful, fabulously-talented ballerinas was enough to inspire the novel but not enough to make it work. The dapper war hero society burglar and stick-up man was not very believable either.

I never elevated myself out of the old pulp fiction bump and grind while in Canada. After completing *The Bandit And The Ballerina* I returned to New York City and resumed writing action-adventure novels, which really wasn't so terrible. In fact, writing pulp fiction was fun most of the time.

The most important lesson I learned in the cabin and surrounding forests concerned my rotten stinking anger. Whenever I became angry when living previously in New York City, I tended to blame someone whom I believed was bothering, insulting or violating me in some unforgivable way.

I also became angry in Canada but couldn't blame anyone because I seldom saw other people. Gradually, painfully, I admitted the unpleasant truth that anger evidently originated within me, provoked by deep-rooted frustrations simmering and rising occasionally to full awful consciousness. So I became angry all by myself. I didn't need other people to tick me off.

That major insight helped me deal with my anger more intelligently, instead of redirecting it toward inno-cent people against whom I might provoke ugly confrontations. I'm surprised no one ever killed me.

All was not insights and outdoor fun when I lived in Canada. Many times I wondered if I was crazy for giving up my steady PR career in order to become a novelist, with all the uncertainties of the freelance life, and living in that falling apart cabin without electricity and plumb-ing. Many times I was tormented by worry about money and whether or not I was a poor deluded fool for thinking I could become a great writer when actually I was a loser who had failed at almost everything I'd ever tried.

Despite periodic self-doubt, self-loathing and all-around confusion, my three years alone in that cabin were among the best of my life. Most of the time I felt clear, pure and in direct touch with fundamental reality. Surrounding Canadian forests were a taste of paradise on earth which made me stronger, more resourceful and more mature. I'd love to live that way again, but with electricity and plumbing this time, although I guess that wouldn't be the same.

We cannot recapture the past except in our minds, although I'd certainly try if I had the bucks to bring it off.

17

THE KOTZWINKLE FACTOR

I WOULD BE REMISS IF I DID NOT MENTION THE importance of William Kotzwinkle to my literary career. He exerted a TREMENDOUS influence on me via incisive literary advice that he gave me over the years. I additionally benefited from exposure to his brilliant imaginative mind.

Bill is best known for writing the novelization of *E.T. The Extraterrestrial* which was the top-selling novel internationally of the 1980s. He also wrote what some consider the finest novel about the 1960s *The Fan Man*, plus numerous other novels and even children's books, one of which, *Walter The Farting Dog*, that he wrote with Glenn Murray and Bill's wife Elizabeth Gundy, also became a best-seller.

I first met Bill early one morning in 1962 on a bus sitting in a terminal in upper Manhattan. The bus contained mostly employees of Prentice-Hall publishing company. Still sleepy, some of us hung over, a few probably stoned, we were going to our jobs at Prentice-Hall headquarters in Englewood Cliffs, New Jersey.

I was a direct-mail advertising copywriter for Prentice-Hall and had taken a seat toward the back of the bus. Gradually the bus filled with people. Then I spotted a guy about five feet six inches tall with long brown beard, wearing a tweedy jacket and tweedy Irish newsboy style cap set at a rakish angle, coming toward me down the center aisle. He looked like a character out of a novel by James Joyce, asked if the empty seat beside me was taken, I said no, and he sat down.

The bus rumbled over the George Washington Bridge toward New Jersey. Bill and I started talking. I learned that he was a copywriter in another department of Prentice-Hall. We soon discovered that we both wanted to become novelists someday. He had majored in English at Penn State and studied under John Barth who was a famous writer of quality literature during that era, now almost completely forgotten.

Thus did Bill and I become friends based on literature. We also were interested in Carl Jung and mystical religious practices. We often hung out together after work. Bill was dating a woman named Elizabeth Gundy who also wanted to become a writer and often hung out with us, and whom he later married.

At Prentice-Hall I became friendly with other guys who wanted to become writers. Occasionally I hung out with them after work hours. They included:

Lin Carter whom I've mentioned several chapters back, who later wrote many published books in the sci-fi and sword and sorcery genres.

Noel Vreeland who later wrote many published gothic horror novels and married Lin.

Alexander Mason who later wrote two published action/adventure novels,

Philippe Coupey who later wrote numerous

published novels including non-fiction books about Zen Buddhism and now is a leader of the Zen movement in Paris.

Nelson Lyon who later wrote for *Saturday Night Live*, went to Hollywood, became a film director, hung out with stars, and was said to be the last person to see John Belushi alive.

Sometime in the 1960s Bill and Elizabeth moved from the Upper West Side to a pad on Christopher Street in Greenwich Village. Often I visited them there. One evening he showed me some stories he had written. I probably was stoned and didn't read them very carefully; they didn't impress me much.

Those stories became part of a collection published in his first book *Elephant Bangs Train*. I read the book which meant reading the same stories over again. That second time around I considered those same stories absolutely magnificent, thoroughly innovative and quite entertaining. I realized to my astonishment that my buddy Bill was a literary genius!

He later wrote and had published *Hermes 3000*, another excellent collection of stories which was named after his typewriter. Then he wrote and had published many novels and story collections, including children's books.

I quit my job and became a writer of novels a few years after Bill quit his job. Bill critiqued many of my novels and taught me much about the art and craft of writing stories. He immediately could zero in on what was wrong with a story and what was right.

Approximately 1972 he and Elizabeth relocated to a remote forest region of Canada. I took over their old apartment on Christopher Street and then, after visiting them in Canada a few times, I relocated there in 1974 to the previously described rundown cabin a few miles from their house.

Bill and I often walked or snowshoed through vast sprawling Canadian forests. Usually there were no trails and we went bushwhacking. A few times we became so engrossed in conversations that we got lost which was scary because it was an immense unfamiliar wilderness, but somehow, we always found our way back to civilization.

We primarily discussed books, writing and abstract philosophy/theology. I found these discussions extraordinarily stimulating intellectually. Knowing Bill was like receiving an education on the graduate level.

I shouldn't admit it in writing, because it is not very complimentary to me, but I was in awe of Bill, the range of his imagination, the depth of his thought, his almost uncanny understanding of everything, and I had to be honest with myself and admit that he was far more intelligent than I.

Finally I returned to New York City. Bill later moved to Maine. Around that time, he wrote the novelization of *E.T. The Extraterrestrial* which transformed his life. I visited him in Maine several times after that and we resumed our wide-ranging hiking and discussions.

Bill influenced me enormously by the quality of his creative imagination, his technical writing skills, and his deep commitment to writing novels, which probably was even deeper than my commitment. When I was thinking of becoming a full-time novelist, he encouraged me to quit my job and take that big step into the unknown. He thought I could bring it off.

He was partially right and partially wrong. I became a novelist but never on his level.

One of my favorites among his novels was *Fata*

Morgana which he dedicated to me. The dedication reads:

For Inspector L.

He often referred to me as "the inspector" because I wrote so many cop books. I always will be grateful for the literary assistance he has given me and for his intellectually stimulating personality. If I never met Bill, I might never have had the courage to take the leap into full time writing. Sometimes I think I'm nothing more than a character in one of his novels.

18

BILL KOTZWINKLE RESPONDS

Dear Inspector L,

Thanks so much for the glowing chapter. It humbled me and made me determined to live up to it.

I was amused by you remembering about John Barth. I actually never took a class with him though we all thought he was IT. A roommate of mine *did* take Barth's writing class. He came to me in despair, saying, "I'm supposed to write a story for Barth but I can't do it." He asked me to write the story for him. I was flunking everything but I could string sentences together, so I wrote a story and my roommate handed it in.

After reading it, Barth told my roommate that he should pursue a career as a writer. This gave us both a good laugh, and I was deeply gratified because in the only writing class I *actually* took at Penn State, Biographical Writing, I got an F. Ron Nowicki, who went on to create the prestigious San Francisco Review, was in the class with me. He got an A. But I had chosen Hemingway as my subject, and I quoted some stuff about Hemingway from Playboy, my favorite magazine at the time. I thought the material I quoted was interesting and pertinent. The teacher laid into me for quoting from Playboy, as if it were a magazine from hell. He berated me openly to the class, much to Nowicki's amusement. And then he flunked me. And his wife flunked me in her art class. The only really good drawing I did for her was of a pair of bongo drums I owned at the time. I was inspired. In a further touch of irony, years later at the San Francisco Review Nowicki gave my novella *Swimmer in the Secret Sea* a glowing review.

My real teacher at Penn State was Gardner Tilson, a graduate theater arts major with whom I roomed at a different time. I was pretty rough around the edges at that time and the only reason he deigned to let me room with him was because he needed the money. For weeks he was rehearsing The Glass Menagerie in our apartment, and I heard him practicing his lines over and over. One day he asked me to cue him, and so I found myself speaking the beautiful language of Tennessee Williams, and it got to me. In fact, it was like a bolt of lightning.

And from you I learned about humor. There's a Len Levinson stream of humor that's always with me. Seeing the ridiculous in ourselves and turning it to humor—that's one of the gifts with which you have entertained me for years, in person and on paper. You long ago mastered the ironic touch. It's one of the reasons a publisher wants to put your observations into a book. It seems as if all along as you wrote your eighty-some books, another book was being prepared in the background—a commentary on the frantic process of writing at inhuman speed. You always laughed about it, saying it was rotting your mind. But I knew it was do or die, and under horrible pressure you turned out a book that sold ninety thousand copies. I was in awe of that and still am.

And then there is the Len Levinson laugh, a marvelous sound I can hear in my head anytime I want to cheer myself up. When you really let loose with it you enter the bird range, a raucous call from the tropics, like the parrot who inspired you to write a novel with a parrot as the hero. Your laugh brightens the life of those who hear it, I can assure you. From the moment I met you, I saw humor was always on your lips and at your fingertips, and I knew that you possessed it in a rare degree, and your laugh was its spontaneous manifestation.

Looking back, the only reason I can see for being a copywriter at Prentice-Hall is that I met you. I certainly didn't fulfill the job. Not one of my sales letters aimed at secretaries was ever deemed good enough to be sent out into the world. But you got a very funny novel out of your time in your Prentice-Hall basement cubicle churning out crazed sales letters for dubious self-help books. I suppose we could say that at least one person was helped by those self-help books—you—because your *Cobra Woman* is filled with high-octane humor, its hero a deranged copywriter.

After writing sales letters, we both quit Prentice-Hall, along with Philippe Coupey, now an esteemed Zen monk in Paris. I always remember his parting line when we quit. He pointed toward the exit and said, "When I go through that door for the last time, ducks will fly out of my ass."

I went on to write articles such as South American Woman Gives Birth to Puppies for *The Midnight Examiner*. And you went on to become a high-powered press agent. I finally quit The Examiner but you held on as a press agent, but I could tell that even though you chaperoned people like John Lennon around New York City, your heart was elsewhere. I was supporting myself with freelance magazine writing which meant I was free to fuck off when I wanted to. So I came to your Lower East Side pad one morning and said, "We've got to get stoned and go to the Metropolitan Museum." By this time I had realized the Met was an engine of tremendous creative energy, with all those ancient artifacts still giving off original vibrations. You were reluctant to join me, but I worked on you while you were getting into your press agent suit and tie. You were an impeccable dresser but I undermined you as you stood before your mirror. Worn down by me, you called the agency and told them you were ill. We went out to have a splendid day among the ancients, and not long after you quit your life as a press agent and took up the wild life of a writer. I never dared disturb you then, because you'd been given impossible deadlines that would have destroyed a weaker mind. To break your concentration with a frivolous visit would have been unpardonable. Here was a man crouched over his typewriter with smoke coming out of his ears.

But on the weekends, though you were pale from lack of sunlight, you were hilarious on the subject of genre writing, for you could work in any genre—tough PIs, Marine combat sergeants, fast-draw cowboys, submarine commanders, racing drivers, anything they threw at you. I remember you saying, "They can't defeat me."

In a dry spell you drove a cab at night, following which you wrote a funny and insightful novel about cabdrivers. You were The Writing Machine Of Manhattan.

By that time you were living in Hell's Kitchen, which seemed a peculiarly correct address for one being boiled alive in the genre stew.

Later you took over our Christopher Street apartment. When we visited you there, the apartment seemed strangely smaller because you had painted the office window black as an aid to concentration. I understood. It had to be done. The pressure was on, as always. Interactions with the outer world were to be kept to a minimum so you could meet another impossible deadline.

While you were being boiled alive in Hell's Kitchen, and painting the window black on Christopher Street, you did what had to be done but I doubt if you realized you were creating a legend, but that's what has happened. A whole new generation has awakened to the fun of your books, to their zany, wild plots and crackling dialogue. I hope this brief reminiscence by yours truly will add to the fun of discovering you.

(Bill refers to a novel of mine called *Cobra Woman*, and another book about a parrot, both of which will be covered in detail later in this book.)

19

MY GREAT AMERICAN HALLUCINATORY NOVEL

I NEVER KEPT A DIARY DURING MY EARLY YEARS AS A writer, so dates and sequences in this book might be a little off. At the age of 85, my past seems like a huge jumble of events, people and questionable decisions. Anyway, to my best recollection, after returning to NYC, one of the first novels I wrote was *Where the Action Is* for Belmont-Tower.

Whenever I delivered a new manuscript to Belmont-Tower, I received my assignment for the next. So one afternoon I was sitting in the office of my editor, the great Peter McCurtin, listening to him describe my new upcoming novel.

Peter seemed very agitated that day, not his usual calm, scholarly demeanor. He said that one of his authors was supposed to deliver a novel in the *Cherry Delight* series by Glen Chase in five (5) days but had fallen sick. The novel was scheduled for publication, and someone needed to write it quickly. He looked into my eyes and asked me to write this novel IN FIVE DAYS!!!

How could I say no to my editor, mentor and literary hero? Peter had written over 100 published novels himself and developed a fabulous, hard-punching, fast-moving literary style which I greatly admired and tried to emulate in books I wrote for him.

The cover for the *Cherry Delight* novel already had been completed. It showed the leading lady Cherry Delight in a metallic gray jumpsuit kneeling on a roulette wheel and aiming a pistol that looked like a Luger at someone to my left. The jacket copy said that an evil criminal genius with occult powers was putting Las Vegas casinos out of business, which could damage the entire U.S. economy. Cherry had to stop him at all costs. The title was *Where the Action Is*.

I carried the cover home to my Hell's Kitchen pad, sat at my desk and wondered how I could possibly write a complete novel based on that ridiculous premise, in only five days. The answer seemed obvious. Drink lots of coffee and drop amphetamine pills that I had lying around.

So I got myself all hyped up and went to work. I didn't have time to think about a plot. I had to start writing immediately whatever rose to the top of my brain. I imagined Cherry on a jumbo jet landing at the airport in Las Vegas, wrote it down and kept banging that keyboard.

I slept very little during those five days. I just kept drinking coffee and popping pills. Everyone knows that lack of sleep causes hallucinations, which means the novel has a certain weird stream of consciousness quality, like a Technicolor surrealist action dream.

Whenever I didn't know what to write next, I tossed in a sex scene or shootout or punchout, and lots of long loopy dialogue. I couldn't stop to think. I needed to write, write, write, if I wanted to make the deadline.

The result is perhaps one of the strangest novels ever written in the history of the world. I can't recommend it to ordinary readers, but psychiatrists, psychologists and students of abnormal psychology might find it of interest.

In a daze I delivered the final manuscript on time to Peter. He thanked me, then I walked home crosstown from Belmont-Tower's Park Avenue South office to my Hell's kitchen hovel, climbed up the shaky ladder of my loft bed, and collapsed into a deep coma. To my best recollection, I slept around 12 hours and was groggy for a few days afterwards. Ah, the romance of being an artist.

Joe Kenney wrote a review of *Where the Action Is* in the August 2012 issue of his *Glorious Trash* blog. He said in the last paragraph:

> Really though, at 176 pages of big print, **Where The Action Is** comes off more like a novella, a breezy read that I finished before I knew it; which, again, is how I think these men's adventure novels should be written. The longer they are, the more prone they are to becoming padded and tiresome. Levinson keeps things moving at a steady, fun clip, but be warned again that this novel is more of a satire and comedy than a **Baroness**-type action novel.

Joe interviewed me in *Paperback Fanatic* magazine #23. When the subject of *Where the Action Is* came up, I told him:

"The vulgarities of this novel probably never will be matched in American Fiction."

   As far as I know, this novel never has been republished in paper or as an ebook, which probably is for the best.

20

INSIDE MY "INSIDE JOB"

MY NOVEL *INSIDE JOB* BY NICHOLAS BRADY, PUBLISHED IN 1978, began like most of my early novels – in the office of editor Peter McCurtin at Belmont-Tower publishing company on Park Avenue South in New York City.

Peter asked if I knew anything about the property room at NYPD headquarters. I replied that I'd heard of it but didn't know much. He said it was loaded with confiscated cash, jewels, drugs, furs, art and other items worth millions of dollars, and asked me to write a novel about a robbery of it by crooked police officers, the inside job indicated by the title.

I remember Peter showing me the artist's sketch of the cover whose copy read: "The NYPD property room, bulging with millions in recovered cash, drugs, and jewels, is ripped off!"

That's what I had to work with. I went home and tried to figure out the story. Who exactly would be the robber cops? Why would they attempt such a dangerous enterprise? How could they pull it off? Would they get caught?

That was when Ed Koch was mayor and NYC was going bankrupt. Hordes of city workers were being laid off including cops, fireman, teachers, sanitation workers, social workers, etc. Crime was rampant. It seemed that NYC had become ungovernable.

In that turbulent atmosphere, I decided the perps would be four angry resentful cops laid off during the budget crisis. One actually had worked in the property room and knew how it functioned. Before the heist went down, I needed to figure out who these cops were as human beings.

Many of my own frustrations and disappointments were heaped onto the shoulders of poor Mike Brody, leader of the cop gang. The media always is regaling us with stories about successful talented winners, but what about losers and failures which is what Brody and the others felt like after getting laid off, and how I often felt in those days and even now.

The four cops: Michael Brody, Anthony Ricci, Dennis Laganello and Robert Hardesty all thought they were very smart guys, but intelligence is not enough when planning a complicated heist because you can't plan for everything. That's why crime doesn't pay most of the time.

The four dismissed cops were blinded by desperation combined with arrogance. They thought they were so smart they could beat the system. Could they?

They weren't intrinsically evil but became so when their worlds shattered. If they hadn't been laid off, they might've enjoyed successful careers in law enforcement. All were very tough guys, but unfortunately too weak to withstand temptation for revenge and big bucks.

I lived in New York City 42 years, arriving when I was 26 and leaving when 68. Now I've relocated to a peaceful little Midwestern town population 3000, surrounded by corn and soybean fields, way out here on the Great American Prairie.

Since living here I've become aware that NYC had a tremendous amount of crime compared to this bucolic small town. When I lived in NYC, often I read in the press about people from all walks of life engaging in major and minor crimes. I even personally met people socially who engaged in illegal activities, and I had been a crime victim myself thirteen times, getting mugged, robbed, apartment burglaries, beat up outside a bar, held up at knifepoint in a doorway of the East Village, etc.

It seemed that many if not most New Yorkers simply did not respect the law, which resulted in New Yorkers from Wall Street to Mulberry Street to 125th Street and all around the town stealing, swindling, mugging and occasionally killing if they thought they could get away with it.

So NYC itself became one of the perps in the novel because of its widespread moral bankruptcy. One needed to be cautious at all times in NYC, otherwise one easily could become a crime victim, unlike this dinky little prairie town where street violence, robbery and burglary are virtually non-existent.

Mayor Rudy Guiliani and Police Commissioner Bill Bratton did the impossible and cleaned up NYC, and Mayor Mike Bloomberg and Police Commissioner Raymond Kelley built upon their success. Now those competent leaders are long gone, and internet websites report the city is sliding back into crime, violence and utter chaos.

If people were honest, we wouldn't need so many police and so much government. But many people aren't honest, and temptation is difficult to withstand in a city where traditional morality is widely considered obsolete if not totally ridiculous.

Joe Kenney wrote a review of *Inside Job* for his *Glorious Trash* blog. Here are excerpts:

> I always figured Len would've turned in a nice '70s crime tale, and he doesn't disappoint, though be aware *Inside Job* takes many of the typical trappings of the heist genre and turns them on their head.
>
> Overall I enjoyed *Inside Job*, and I'd say it's definitely worth reading for the Len Levinson fan, or someone looking for an unusual take on a '70s crime novel.

It's me Lenny talking again. Many years before I wrote *Inside Job*, I read *Crime and Punishment* by Fyodor Dostoyevsky twice, perhaps twenty years apart, and probably will read it again someday. In his novel Dostoyevsky explored the convoluted mind of a mentally disturbed murderer who imagined he was above good and evil, in an atmosphere of doom and gloom on the murky streets of old Moscow.

Crime and Punishment influenced *Inside Job* considerably, infusing it with the same grim sense of moral corruption and danger of getting caught. *Inside Job* is not a happy upbeat novel or razzle dazzle adventure, but hard-core realistic tragedy concerning a daring crime and its devastating aftermath.

Inside Job has been republished as both ebooks and paperbacks under my real name Len Levinson, and available for anyone who might want a gritty psychological drama about ordinary decent people like you and me driven by cruel circumstances to become thieves and murderers.

21

MY STRANGE CAREER AS A
WOMAN WRITER (PART ONE)

MY NOVEL SWEETER THAN CANDY BY CYNTHIA WILKERSON began one afternoon in 1977 when I sat in an editorial office of Belmont-Tower in New York City, beside the desk of an editor named Milburn Smith. I don't remember where my usual editor Peter McCurtin was that day.

Milburn was in his 30s, around 6 feet 4 inches tall, slim, rawboned, long face with rugged features. Like many editors he dressed like a college professor, or perhaps college professors dressed like book editors.

Usually my BT editors asked me to write another razzle-dazzle action/adventure novel with people shooting, stabbing, punching and kicking each other, but on the afternoon in question, Milburn asked me to write something quite different, a novel similar to one on the best-seller lists those days: *Blue Skys, No Candy* by Gael Greene.

Blue Skys, No Candy was a big hit much discussed in the media as a sensationally erotic breakthrough in feminist literature. A friend referred to it as *"Blue Skys, No*

Panties". Ms. Greene also was a well-known restaurant critic for *NEW YORK* magazine.

In plain English, Milburn wanted me to rip off *Blue Skys, No Candy*.

After leaving Milburn, I bought a copy of *Blue Skys, No Candy*, carried it home, read it front to back, and evaluated it as pedestrian middlebrow smut. My only reasonable response was to out-smut Gael Greene, a challenge for which I felt fully qualified given my smutty brain during my younger days.

I'd need a female pseudonym and somehow my mind brought to the surface *Cynthia Wilkerson*. I also invented the title *Sweeter Than Candy* which I considered a wonderfully clever response to *Blue Skies, No Candy* which itself was a response to another breakthrough feminist erotic novel, *Fear Of Flying* by Erica Jong

It was fun to write a novel under a woman's name, from a woman's point of view. While working on it, I was led to the seemingly obvious conclusion that women really aren't that different from men in many ways, such as ambition, overall sex drive, and occasional ruthlessness to get what they want, although women certainly look and dress differently, and have what a lady friend of mine called "the egg role" i.e. the potential to get pregnant. Women usually are much more subtle than men, which probably makes them more dangerous.

In 2014 I re-read *Sweeter Than Candy* for the first time since I delivered the manuscript in 1977. I re-read it because Joe Kenney of the *Glorious Trash* blog asked me to write a brief commentary to accompany a review he was writing.

As I re-read *Sweeter Than Candy*, it seemed that the novel was approximately 30% percent hard core erotica spiced with zany comedic overtones. The rest is satire on

NYC snobbery and pretentiousness, also spiced with zany comedic overtones.

A few times I laughed out loud at my own words written around 37 years ago. The sexually voracious lead character Vivian Sinclair, drama critic for a daily newspaper, is hilarious in her hypocrisy, silliness, self-deception and ruthless ambition, yet also is somewhat sympathetic because all she really wants is true love, although having no idea what it is (and neither did Cynthia Wilkerson for that matter). Vivian Sinclair's primary loyalty was to her last orgasm.

I did not intend to condemn all NYC women in this novel. The overwhelming majority whom I met were delightful to know, clear-headed, down to earth, hardworking, respectful of others, usually more intelligent and honorable than I, and some gave me excellent advice over the years.

My character and target Vivian Sinclair did not represent this admirable class of women. Vivian was the basic female phony, and we all know they exist as do male phonies. In fact, I have been a phony baloney myself at times, such as masquerading as a woman when I wrote *Sweeter Than Candy*.

The plot held my attention with its unexpected twists and turns spiked with crackling dialogue. Regrettably there are many typos, but BT was not known for copy editing prowess. For example, on page 196, a Greenwich Village bar was referred to as Nebraska Midnight. On page 198 it had become Dakota Midnight. Such errors must have been very disconcerting for readers. That particular bar was based on the Montana Eve saloon on the west side of 7th Avenue north of Sheridan Square, where my half-brother worked as bartender and then manager for a while, and where I visited occasionally.

Please forgive my immodesty but I'm proud to say that *Sweeter Than Candy* actually was much more smutty than *Blue Skies, No Candy*, and a better read as well. Unfortunately, *Sweeter Than Candy* never was embraced by the New York literati, went out of print long ago, and never republished as far as I know.

Joe Kenney reviewed *Sweeter Than Candy* for his *Glorious Trash* blog on 12/11/14. Among other remarks, he said:

> At 265 pages, not only is **Sweeter Than Candy** one of the longer books of Len's I've yet read, it's also by far the most trashy, sleazy, and explicit. Like (Gael) Greene's novel, this one is narrated by its female (anti)hero: Vivian Sinclair, the 35 year-old "sexual terror of Manhattan" who makes her living as a drama critic for a small New York newspaper.
>
> Len's writing is as ever strong and enjoyable; there are tons of lines and pieces of dialog that are rife for quoting, but I'm a lazy man. He covers all the bases from the sleazy to the profound. He does though slip in and out of present tense at times, which makes for an awkward read given that the novel is in past tense. Also, the book is littered with typos and misprintings, though this isn't Len's doing; it's the usual subpar Belmont Tower "editing" at work.
>
> This is not to take away from the novel itself, which is a fun and sleazy romp through late 1970s New York City. As I read it, it occurred to me that **Sweeter Than Candy** was yet another of Len's novels that would've gotten a lot more attention if it had been published by an outfit with better distribution - the very scarcity of **Sweeter Than Candy** suggests that it likely had a small

print run. It's a shame, really, as the novel deserved a better fate.

I agree with Joe that the novel deserved a better fate, or perhaps it truly received the fate it deserved. I've often wondered how Cynthia's readers would react if they knew that she had grown a beard.

22

MY VERY FIRST WAR NOVEL

How could a mild-mannered, philosophical dude like me write 35 war novels?

The truth is I'm fascinated by war probably because I was raised on it, only four years old when Germany invaded Poland, only six when Japan bombed Pearl Harbor.

Growing up in Massachusetts, my mind regularly was filled with sensational war news including periodic reports of local men killed and wounded. Often it seemed that the Allies were losing, and America would become occupied by fanatical Nazi mass murderers and/or Japanese head-choppers.

The home front was not disconnected from the war. Metal and paper collections were common, ration books issued, air raid drills occurring regularly in schools, women working in factories, and victory by no means certain. An atmosphere of desperation pervaded the land, intensified by many serious reversals including one-third of the U.S. battle fleet demolished at Pearl Harbor.

Not only was World War Two impacting me daily, my father was a World War One veteran, having served with the famed Second Division in six major battle engagements, wounded at Chateau-Thierry. A two-inch diameter sunburst scar was visible near his left temple to his dying day.

We lived together, my mother having passed on when I was four. Pops managed our apartment like a barracks, he the sergeant and I the private. He imposed strict discipline and backed it with threats of physical violence including a few incidents of actual physical violence, but it wasn't all bad because I learned valuable coping skills at an early age, which perhaps was his purpose all along.

As my reading skills improved and mind matured, I read many articles and books about war. I wanted to know how and why nations went to war, and how and why soldiers could bring themselves to kill total strangers. I also wondered how I'd behave in war. Would I follow orders and do my duty or throw away my rifle and run for the hills?

I enlisted in the Army in 1954 at age 19, because I wanted the G.I. Bill for college. It was during the Korean War. Peace talks were underway at Panmunjom so I assumed the war would end officially soon and I'd enjoy a peaceful military career in some exotic post like Tokyo, wearing my snazzy Ike jacket, surrounded by beautiful women.

Instead, we trainees were taught that North Koreans and Chicoms were treacherous, the ceasefire wouldn't last, and we'd better pay attention to instructors because our next assignments probably would be the front line in Korea, with actual bullets whizzing through the air, and real artillery shells bursting nearby.

During training I fired .30 and .50 caliber machine

guns, threw live hand grenades, fired bazookas, became semi-deafened occasionally by artillery blasts, followed huge, lumbering tanks into mock attacks, and crawled across the muddy infiltration course at night, live machine gun fire overhead. I learned that war was not at all glorious, but dirty, noisy, bloody, brutal and grotesque for frontline soldiers.

Sergeants thoroughly indoctrinated us in the combat mentality. Often I fantasized killing people, or me getting machine gunned, or blown to bits by an artillery shell. Soldiers were trained to follow orders instantly, without thinking. I fell in line like virtually all young soldiers because hellhole stockades seemed far worse. Throwing away my rifle and running for the hills was unthinkable.

I lived in fear of stockades, where a newcomer would be warmly welcomed with a blanket party consisting of a blanket thrown over him, and everyone punched and kicked the blanket, while guards looked the other way. I personally met soldiers who'd been in stockades and confirmed these practices.

After training I was assigned to the 53rd Infantry Regiment at Fort Richardson in Alaska, becoming an ordinary foot soldier carrying a Browning Automatic Rifle (BAR) which was heavy, cumbersome, and tended to jam. About six months later I was transferred to the 4th Engineers who were combat engineers constantly training to build or blow up bridges and other structures in hotspots, and laying and detecting minefields, often at night. The British call such soldiers sappers.

We Alaskan snow soldiers continually were reminded forcefully that we stood only 20 minutes jet time from Siberia. A Russian parachute division or two could drop on us at any moment, so we'd be better prepared at all times to ride trucks into the tundra to fight and defend the most important military asset in the area: Elmendorf Air Force Base adjacent to Fort Richardson.

Incessant frenzied preparation for imminent battle produced lots of anxious young guys with rifles running, skiing or riding in trucks around the landscape on training exercises. We definitely acquired the combat mentality, prepared to kill on command.

I too became highly stressed, and late one evening in a Quonset hut on the outskirts of Fort Richardson, got into an altercation with a soldier from Buffalo, New York, who was built like a buffalo.

I didn't know this guy well, but evidently, he didn't like me. I don't know why he didn't like me but occasionally I was a wise guy and smart aleck and evidently said or did something that pissed him off.

On the evening in question, as I lay comatose on my back on my bunk, in fatigues but no boots, he walked up to my bunk and kicked one of the legs. I told him if he kicked it again, I'd get up and punch him in the mouth. He kicked it again. I laced on my boots, walked up to him, and he raised his hands, ready to rumble. He seemed surprised that I was facing him, because he probably weighed around 75 pounds more than I, perhaps four inches taller with a longer reach. He also was semi-drunk on PX beer, slowing his reflexes, enabling me to land the first punch, a solid left jab to his face, which rocked him on his heels.

If I had possessed the true killer instinct, I would have zeroed in for the kill, throwing hard punches from all angles, and knocked him out, but as a half-baked intellectual, became amazed at the sight of him backpedaling, trying to clear his head. I thought: Wow – did I really hit him that hard?

As I marveled at my own strength, the buffalo regained full consciousness and proceeded to throw a flurry of solid punches with his big fists, completely overwhelming me with his size and strength, finally knocking me out, causing headaches for around a month. The lesson learned was that if I ever got into another fight, I should never let up until my opponent was unconscious. But I never had another fist fight to this day.

During my three-year enlistment I met many veterans of World War Two still on active duty. One of my sergeants had survived the Bataan Death March. After a few beers or during chow while on maneuvers, sometimes old sergeants spoke of war experiences. All were very tough guys. Many actually had killed people. I admired them greatly and still do.

After mustering out, I attended Michigan State University on the GI Bill and signed up for many history courses, which meant reading more about war. After graduating with a B.A. in 1961, I continued war research in my spare time.

When I became a novelist in 1971, naturally I wanted to write a war novel. One afternoon circa 1977, while sitting in the office of Milburn Smith, my editor at Belmont-Tower, who had replaced my usual editor Peter McCurtin, we were discussing what I should write next. I told him I wanted to write a war novel. He smiled and said something like: "Sounds like a good idea."

I walked home to my Hell's Kitchen studio pad, sat at my desk, and wondered what kind of war novel to write. There were so many possibilities. Finally I decided to set my first war novel during the most dramatic battle during World War Two in the European Theater of Operations. But many dramatic battles were fought in Europe. My top two choices were the D-Day Normandy Beach landings or the Battle of the Bulge. Finally, the latter won out.

I saw in my mind's eye a platoon of American soldiers caught up in the middle of the German onslaught on the very first page, because it's always best to start an action novel with action – what else? And naturally the platoon would be led by a badass sergeant like the badass sergeants I served under.

Sergeant Mazursky was partially based on a friend of mine named Mike Nichols who'd been a World War II combat veteran and former convict for eight years in a federal penitentiary for smuggling drugs now legal in many states. He was eight years older than I, a tough guy ready to rumble at all times, reminding me of my father, but we got along well for some strange reason.

Mike told me once: "You're the craziest person I ever met in my life, but you *seem* normal."

I considered that a very great compliment because Mike had travelled extensively and met many crazy people.

Often I hung out with him in Greenwich Village where he and his wife Maggie lived on Hudson Street, and I lived nearby at 347 West 4th Street. He influenced me considerably for better or worse but died in 1993. A framed photograph of him stares as me as I write these words.

I never wanted to sanitize or glamorize war but believed that unheralded acts of heroism are common at the front, because soldiers tend to look out for each other. They also develop sardonic senses of humor rather than go bonkers.

During wartime, combatants tend to hate each other. For the sake of accuracy, these wrathful attitudes are reproduced faithfully in all my war novels, which might jolt sensibilities of gentle souls who believe everyone should love everyone.

I dreamed up the title *Doom Platoon* because the platoon quickly became outnumbered, surrounded and truly seemed doomed. Many actually were killed.

The completed novel was published by Belmont-Tower in 1978. My pseudonym Richard Gallagher was based on the name of an acquaintance when I lived in Canada.

Doom Platoon always will occupy a special place in my heart because it was my first war novel. Subsequently I wrote 34 more. Thankfully, *Doom Platoon* has been republished in paperback and as ebooks under my real name Len Levinson, for anyone wanting to experience frontline combat during the Battle of the Bulge, from the comfort and safety of his (or her) easy chair.

23

MY STRANGE CAREER AS A
WOMAN AUTHOR (PART TWO)

MY BELMONT TOWER EDITOR IN 1978 STILL WAS
Milburn Smith, tall, lanky. probably in his thirties,
dressed like a banker or lawyer or college professor with
jacket off. One day we were sitting in his office, tossing
around ideas for my next novel. In the midst of conversation, he slowly turned away from me, leaned back in
his chair, stared into space for around twenty seconds,
appeared deep in thought, then turned to me again and
said: "Let's bring back Cindy. She was a good old gal."

Those were his exact words to my best recollection.
Strange how some conversations or incidents remain in
our memories forever, while others equally or perhaps
more important are forgotten.

Who in the world was Cindy? He was referring to
none other than Cynthia Wilkerson. And who in the
world was Cynthia Wilkerson?

None other than I myself, your not-so-humble corre-
spondent. I previously had written a novel for Milburn
called *Sweeter Than Candy* by Cynthia Wilkerson, already
mentioned. It was a response to *Blue Skies, No Candy* by

Gael Greene, the latter a massive best-seller about a sexually-active, ultra-modern New York woman.

Milburn specified a word count much longer than usual for this new Cynthia Wilkerson novel, around 100,000 words so they could charge a higher price. Evidently *Sweeter Than Candy* was selling well enough to justify another Cynthia Wilkerson extravaganza.

So I walked home from Milburn's office to my deteriorating studio apartment hovel in Hell's Kitchen, wondering what to write about.

Lying on my broken-down sofa, staring at paint peeling from the water-stained ceiling, letting my mind wander, I decided to invade territory occupied by Jacqueline Susann, Danielle Steele, Jackie Collins and all the other literary soap opera queens, and beat them at their own game.

I was determined to write a contemporary women's romance that would surpass anything they'd done, thus propelling myself to the top of the best-seller lists, earning millions of dollars for myself and my various insatiable appetites, and finally moving out of my Hell's Kitchen hovel to a luxurious pad on Central Park South.

Then I made what might have been my first big mistake. I had long been interested in Grand Prix racing and decided to set the narrative against that glamorous international background. It didn't occur to me that potential women readers of *The Fast Life* probably weren't as passionate about exotic cars as I.

If I had any brains, which we all know I don't, I would have set the narrative in the movie world in which I'd been a press agent, which also was the world of Jackie Collins. But I'd recently written a novel about that world titled *Hype!* by Leonard Jordan and didn't want to travel that road again so soon.

For Grand Prix racing research, I had long subscribed to *Road & Track* magazine and knew the subject fairly well. Like most men I was fascinated by cars and still am. One of my best friends had raced on the same Porsche team as Paul Newman. Sports car racing seemed incredibly exciting and sexy because lots of gorgeous international jet set groupies were on the scene.

I hadn't visited Europe yet in person but had seen many European films directed by Federico Fellini, Francois Truffaut, Michelangelo Antonioni, Alain Resnais, Luchino Visconti, René Clément, Jean-Luc Godard, Robert Bresson, etc., and thought I understood the milieu very well.

So I sat down and wrote *The Fast Life* about my ideal type of woman at the time, a romantic fantasy who transmogrified into a beautiful ambitious young blonde American named Veronica Woodward or Roni for short, whose brother had been a NASCAR driver, and she'd also driven NASCAR racing vehicles. As the novel opens, she's touring Europe with a cousin, meets a famous Italian racing car driver at a Paris café, they fall madly and hopelessly in love, and eventually he helps her get into Grand Prix racing.

Mind you, I was writing this novel long before Danica Patrick was born. Once again, I was years ahead of my time.

In 2015, Joe Kenney asked me to write an essay about *The Fast Life* to accompany a review he was writing for his *Glorious Trash* blog. So I read *The Fast Life* for the first time in around 37 years, and to my astonishment actually considered it amazingly wonderful. In fact, it was so great I couldn't believe I wrote it!

That's not to say it's perfect. It's far from perfect. Its

main problem is too many sentences carrying unnecessary words. I should have tightened those sentences, or perhaps they were tighter in my original manuscript, but line editors added words to comply with arcane grammatical rules no longer considered necessary by me. In addition, there were several examples of dialogue too clever, arch, glib and lengthy for their own good.

I was pleased to notice that *The Fast Life* lacked the vulgarity that was the hallmark of many of my early novels, which probably undermined their successes in the marketplace. Evidently I tried to take the high road with *The Fast Life* but that doesn't mean the narrative lacks romantic interludes, because eros is an important component of most people's lives.

I'm also pleased to report that *The Fast Life* is as melodramatic and lurid as any other Len Levinson novel, but thankfully not in the sewer like some of them. In my opinion, the narrative moves swiftly and never slacks off, which was the goal of all my 86 published novels.

I was especially pleased to notice that Roni was a complex tormented character with dark secrets, not just a silly young chickie with delusions of grandeur. Having not looked at the novel for so long, I forgot its twists and turns and how it ended. After 37 years, I thought it suspenseful, realistic and psychologically engaging – I couldn't put it down. The actual racetrack scenes were especially exhilarating. What a wonderful movie it would make.

A feminist might ask indignantly: How can a man possibly write from a woman's viewpoint? My response is that I believe women aren't so different from men when it comes to ambition, sex drive and morality or the lack of it. Women just express these qualities somewhat differently. Usually they have more grace and subtlety than most men. Sometimes women can be as cold-blooded, brutal and diabolical as men, according to my observations and experiences over the years, not to mention contemplation of the character of Lady Macbeth. To paraphrase something Norman Mailer once wrote, if you don't believe men can write realistically about women, you don't believe in the power of art.

I admit that I'm proud of this novel. With slightly better editing, classier cover and more prestigious publisher who promoted it effectively, it might have sold a few hundred thousand copies and accelerated my career in an entirely new affluent direction.

Joe Kenney wrote in his *Glorious Trash* review:

The second of two novels Len Levinson wrote as Cynthia Wilkerson, *The Fast Life* is nothing at all like its predecessor, *Sweeter Than Candy*. Whereas that earlier novel was a sleazy yet goofy tale of a Manhattan-based harlot, this novel is more akin to a category romance, or at the very least something like Jacqueline Susann might've written. It's also longer than the average Belmont Tower book of the day, coming in at only 318 pages but with fairly small print.

Like *Sweeter Than Candy*, *The Fast Life* features a female protagonist, but this novel is told in third person. Our hero is Roni Woodward, a 22-year-old blonde knockout from Savannah, Georgia who has just graduated college and is taking a leisurely tour of Europe with her wallflower of a cousin. On the first page of the novel Roni is in Paris and meets Chaz Razzoni, an Italian in his 40s who is an internationally famous Grand Prix racer, though Roni never heard of him.

I enjoyed *The Fast Life*, but it really is a different kind of novel for Len, as different in its own way as (his) *Cabby* and *Operation Perfidia* were in theirs, though I enjoyed *The Fast Life* more than either of them.

Sometimes I think Joe understands my books better than I.

The Fast Life did not earn millions of dollars for myself and my various insatiable appetites, but at least it has been republished under my real name in paperback and as ebooks for those who might want to speed around the Grand Prix circuit in the 1970s, and experience decadent posh European parties and smoky cafe society of that special era, which has become known as La Dolce Vita, the sweet life, although it wasn't always sweet and could be quite harrowing according to European movies and *The Fast Life*.

24

MY VERY FIRST SERIES

AFTER WRITING SEVERAL NOVELS IN SERIES CREATED BY publishing companies, and after writing a few stand-alone novels, I decided for the first time to create and write my very own series. The year was 1978 and I was 43 years old, living in Manhattan's Hell's Kitchen neighborhood.

What should my first series be? I soon realized that I probably could not write something totally original because every type of cop, spy, Western and other series already had been done to death. That meant I'd need to emulate someone else's series, so I might as well rip off the absolute best. What was the absolute best?

The James Bond series by Ian Fleming – what else? I'd read all the James Bond novels available at that time and enjoyed them because they were unique, freaky, sexy, satirical and rather bizarre, just what the world needed in those days and even today.

I first heard of James Bond during the early days of the John F. Kennedy administration when JFK was reported by the media as a big fan of James Bond. And my previously mentioned friend Lin Carter also was a big James Bond fan and recommended him to me.

While planning my new series, I had to face the truth about myself. I could never be Ian Fleming or even come close because I wasn't a British gentleman, son of a member of parliament, never attended Eton. never was a naval intelligence officer, never had love affairs with titled ladies, never even went to Europe (yet).

I was only Lenny Levinson living in the Hell's Kitchen neighborhood of New York City and had to do James Bond my way, which was the American way. I'd recently seen *Gone with the Wind* for approximately the fourth time, one of my all-time favorite flicks, and decided my James Bond would be named Butler, a descendent of Rhett Butler. My Butler also was from Georgia but unlike Rhett, had graduated from the University of Georgia and been a Green Beret officer in the Nam.

Instead of an elegant British gentleman like Bond James Bond, I envisioned a rowdy all-American sex degenerate who also was brave, intelligent, resourceful, with a big sense of irony and bigger sense of humor. It was with high hopes that I began writing this series.

Unfortunately, my high hopes were sunk yet again by the book-buying marketplace. Butler did not sell well, I'm sorry to say. Why? In order to answer that perplexing question, let me tell the following true story:

In 2016 Joe Kenney emailed me and said he wanted to review my first Butler novel for his *Glorious Trash* blog. He asked me to write an article about the series to accompany his review.

I thought I'd just sit down and write my reminiscences, because I didn't feel like taking time to read all six Butler books, but finally decided I wouldn't do justice to Joe or Butler if I didn't actually read the novels.

So I read them all in around five days and must confess that I wasn't very happy with what I found.

The main problem with *Butler*, from my perspective around 40 years later, was dirty rotten stinking politics. I'm embarrassed to confess that I was a deeply committed Marxist-Leninist-Trotskyite-Communist lunatic during the 1970s, and these poisonous principles occasionally spilled over into the Butler books. Too many paragraphs read as if written by Karl Marx on acid, or Vladimir Lenin on shrooms, or Joseph Stalin on crack cocaine, or Mao Tse Tung on hashish.

The great Leo Tolstoy said: "I have found that a story leaves a deeper impression when it is impossible to tell which side the author is on." I agree completely because stories become tendentious and boring when the author is as politically preachy as I was in *Butler*.

Butler also contains numerous long meandering conversations that should have been cut drastically. There also are numerous long meandering sex scenes which I had thought would make the series more appealing to the sex maniac market but now think made the series too vulgar and helped doom it to failure.

However, I must say in my defense that there also are many wonderfully funny scenes in the *Butler* series, much scintillating dialogue, and numerous genuinely weird situations that you won't read anywhere else.

My favorite novel in the series was #2 *Smart Bombs*, with #4 *Chinese Roulette* a close second. And I'm proud of some of the peculiar characters I invented such as F.J. Shankham, the sinister double-crossing CIA director; Wilma B. Willoughby, Butler's on again off again spy girlfriend; and the quite dignified Madame Wang, owner and CEO of numerous international enterprises which together were called the Kinki Corporation, and who formerly was a prostitute known as Hong Kong Sally.

I also liked the plot of #5 *Love Me to Death*, about militant man-hating feminists screwing prominent wealthy older men to death by employing ancient arcane Persian vaginal manipulation techniques, but then those crazy chicks run into Butler whose prodigious sexual abilities were more than a match for them. This novel is unbelievably lewd, incredibly politically-incorrect, and could not be published today although I think many scenes are hilarious.

I'm no longer the person who wrote the *Butler* series. I no longer advocate violent Communist revolution. I no longer write extended hardcore erotic scenes. And I'm more inclined to cut meaningless dialogue.

The first few books in the *Butler* series were republished under my real name as ebooks a few years ago but the series was cancelled due to weak sales, repeating an all-too-common feature of my so-called literary career. Yet I have read on the internet that many people enjoyed the *Butler* books, which indicates I wasn't totally misguided.

25

MY FIRST WAR SERIES

IN 1979 I WAS LIVING IN A DETERIORATING OLD apartment building in New York City's Hell's Kitchen neighborhood. One day I received a phone call from a man I'd never heard of before, who identified himself as Jim Bryans, a paperback packager. He said that he'd heard of me, read a few of my books and wanted me to write for him.

What is a paperback packager? Jim developed concepts for series and sold them to publishing companies. He then hired writers like me to write actual books, he and or his staff edited them, he hired artists who painted covers for all novels in the series, he probably wrote cover copy, hired someone to do production work, and finally delivered completed packages to publishers who only needed to print, distribute and market them.

Jim invited me to his office to discuss details further. Naturally I went because I had no source of income beside writing novels quickly one after the other. In essence I was a trapeze act without a net.

Jim's office consisted of one-desk in a small private room located in a complex of similar private rooms in an office building somewhere in the East 40s or 50s. He was around six feet six inches tall, broad shoulders, well-fed, short beard, probably fifty-something. He explained that he was a former Dell executive who'd branched off into his own operation. I spoke a bit about myself, then out of the blue he asked: "Have you ever written a World War Two novel?

I replied that indeed I had written a World War Two novel called *Doom Platoon* by Richard Gallagher, set during the Battle of the Bulge, published by Belmont-Tower in 1978.

Jim said that a publisher contact of his was looking for someone to write a World War Two series. Jim asked me to bring him a copy of *Doom Platoon* which he would submit to the publisher. I did so ASAP and a few weeks later Jim called to say the publisher wanted to meet me.

The publisher was Walter Zacharius who together with Roberta Grossman owned Zebra Publishing, their offices on Park Avenue South around 32nd Street. I think Jim attended the meeting, but Walter and I did most of the talking. Walter told me he'd liked *Doom Platoon* and wanted me to write something similar as a series. He also said that he'd been in the Quartermaster Corps during World War Two, rose to the rank of sergeant, and had participated in the liberation of Paris.

In turn I mentioned that I enlisted in the Army in 1954, served three years in the Infantry and Corps of Engineers during the Cold War, was stationed in Alaska for over half of my enlistment, therefore I knew basic military life up close and personal although I'd never been in a hot war. I also said that infantry weapons during my Army years were identical to those used during World War Two, or modified somewhat, and main principles of fire and maneuver were pretty much the same. I assured Walter that I could write about World War Two with a high degree of authenticity although I'd never been there.

I agreed to Walter's deal, probably signed the contract then and there, walked home to my broken-down pad in Hell's Kitchen and tried to figure whether the series should focus on one person or on a unit like a platoon. Finally, I decided on one person who would be a tough sergeant similar to Sergeant Mazursky in *Doom Platoon*.

Mazursky had been based loosely on my friend Mike Nichols whom I've mentioned earlier in this book. Mike had been a World War Two veteran and very badass guy eight years older than I. He had been ready to rumble at any moment and demonstrated no fear or caution when any conflict arose. Occasionally he threw shocking temper tantrums in public and seemed ready to punch out people. Physical intimidation was perfectly okay with him, but we usually got along well, and he became one of my most significant mentors, for better or worse.

Mike's military career had not exactly been illustrious. He went AWOL numerous times during World War Two in Europe, had broken out of a stockade, and instead of fighting for his country full time, had been wheeling and dealing in black markets of France and Germany.

After mustering out, Mike attended Columbia University for a year or two, then dropped out to sell marijuana and become something of a gigolo. He got arrested at the Mexican/Texas border for smuggling marijuana and served eight years in a federal prison during which he wrote for and helped edit the prison newspaper. I met him shortly after he was released in 1961, the same year I arrived in New York City.

Mike was a very complicated guy. He could be vicious or extraordinarily gentle and kind. He could insult you savagely, then take you to dinner. He could cruelly put you down, then burst into laughter as if it was all a big joke. A deeply devoted party animal, he also was a heavy drinker and doper. Cocaine was his drug of choice. He did not believe in God, had Communist inclinations, was surprisingly well read and could talk like an educated man, which he was, or growl like a gangster, which he also was.

He also was amazingly successful with women although not exceptionally good-looking in my opinion. He vaguely resembled the actor Victor Mature combined with John Garfield, Rocky Marciano and Sylvester Stallone. He always had girlfriends even after he got married.

Once I asked him the secret of his success with women. He replied that women were attracted to confident men, but mainly just wanted to be loved. He certainly was very confident and actually seemed to love all the women with whom he was involved.

Another time he said to me: "You're the craziest person I ever met in my life, but you *seem* normal."

I mentioned this before but mention it again because I considered it perhaps the greatest compliment of my life. I had met many of Mike's friends and indeed many were quite crazy. I felt proud to be ranked more crazy than they.

Mike was a first-class conversationalist, raconteur and storyteller. Often I listened to him, spellbound, although his wife Maggie said he never let facts get in the way of a good story.

Mike introduced me to my first wife, a Cuban immigrant whom he called Chi-Chi. Our marriage was stormy and ended in divorce after four years because we simply weren't compatible. During a period of post-divorce angst, I blamed Mike for my misery. "If it hadn't been for you, I never would have met Chi-Chi," I told him angrily.

Mike replied with a winsome smile, "I only introduced you to Chi-Chi. I never told you to marry her."

Of course he was right. My bad judgement was the cause of my unhappiness. I knew that Chi-Chi and I weren't compatible but was dazzled by her beauty and couldn't think clearly, as happened often during my younger days. She became the inspiration for my novel *Cobra Woman* which I'll discuss later.

Mike became inspiration for my new central character Sergeant Mahoney, and I decided to call the series *The Sergeant*. I don't remember where the pseudonym Gordon Davis came from. It might have been invented by Walter.

I was very excited about writing this series because I had been interested in war since childhood, as mentioned previously. I thought my background growing up during World War Two, and three years in the Army, were ideal preparation for writing a World War Two land battle series. My next big literary decision concerned when to start the action, but the answer seemed obvious. Since I already used the Battle of the Bulge in *Doom Platoon*, I began this series with the D-Day landings in Normandy and then would move each novel forward chronologically.

What would the first plot be? I didn't want to write about actual landings and subsequent grinding fight for the beachhead because it had been done in movies numerous times, most notably *The Longest Day*. Instead, I dreamed up a suspenseful commando style mission behind enemy lines to blow up a critical bridge that supported trains carrying German soldiers and equipment to the front.

I wrote in a state of deep intellectual and emotional involvement, and around six weeks later submitted the completed manuscript to Walter, certain that he'd like it. A short while later he invited me to his office, told me that in fact he did like the novel and would publish it *but* he pointed out that ordinary soldiers never went on commando missions behind enemy lines, and he wanted upcoming novels to be about ordinary soldiers engaged in standard World War Two front line battle action. I said okay and that's what I gave him in the next eight novels in the series.

I loved the cover for the first *Sergeant*. It really stood out on bookstore shelves. Ensuing *Sergeant* covers were similar. Walter really understood marketing and that's why Zebra was the most successful privately owned publishing company in America.

Looking back, I think *The Sergeant* series marked a turning point in my literary career. Somehow, I gained a more comprehensive understanding of novel writing while working on its plots, subplots and characters. It was the second series that I created, the first being *Butler* for Belmont-Tower, but *The Sergeant* turned out to be much higher quality than *Butler*. Many readers have praised *The Sergeant* in blogs and on Facebook, which has been most gratifying.

The Sergeant Series has been republished as ebooks by Len Levinson.

26

"THE SERGEANT" TRANSFERS
TO BANTAM

ONE DAY CIRCA 1980, SHORTLY AFTER I'D WRITTEN MY 3rd novel in *The Sergeant* series (titled *Bloody Bush*, about the Battle of the Hedgerows), Walter invited me to dinner at the Palm Restaurant, an expensive prestigious steak house near the United Nations in New York City.

Also attending this fabulous feast was Jim Bryans, the paperback packager who initially introduced me to Walter, and Roberta Grossman who was Walter's business partner. Walter and Roberta owned Zebra/Kensington, the most successful privately-held book publishing operation in America at that time.

After initial pleasantries, and after we ordered, Walter made an astonishing statement. He said that he'd just negotiated a deal with Bantam to publish forthcoming novels in *The Sergeant* series! Then he made an even more astonishing statement, namely that *The Sergeant* and Bantam probably would make me a millionaire!

That latter remark coming suddenly out of nowhere literally blew my mind. I sat there stunned, unable to speak. Walter perhaps thought I'd dropped acid before coming to the restaurant and was having a powerful psychedelic experience. But I hadn't dropped, smoked or shot up anything. I was hallucinating the new black Corvette I was going to buy, with red leather upholstery, largest available engine and four on the floor. I also hallucinated a spacious new apartment in the West 60s near both Lincoln Center and Central Park, an all-new high end stereo system, new suits from Brooks Brothers, plus a cabin in the Catskill Mountains where I could escape from the world whenever I felt the need.

Bantam had tremendous marketing power in those days. *The Sergeant* would be in virtually every bookstore, drugstore, airport, bus terminal and supermarket in America. It appeared that soon I would become a literary star, a dream come true. I might even get interviewed on the Johnny Carson Show, and date movie stars, Vogue models and Broadway dancers.

Oh, the webs we weave ...

Soon after the dinner, Walter arranged a meeting between me and a Bantam executive in his (Walter's) office. I don't remember the Bantam exec's name, but she was in her 30s, blonde, quite good-looking, very well dressed in conservative women's corporate style.

You know how it is. Sometimes people just don't have good chemistry. Perhaps I felt intimidated or afraid of her because she had power over me, since she was in a position to help or impede my literary career. She seemed distant, supercilious, even haughty, as if I were her underling which in fact I was in the publishing hierarchy.

At one point Walter had to do something elsewhere, leaving the lady and me alone in his office. In retrospect I think he figured we might be attracted to each other and could want to have a personal conversation during which I'd ask her to dinner.

Nothing could be further from reality. I felt very uncomfortable in the presence of this aloof woman, and perhaps she felt uncomfortable due to deficient social skills which she covered up with condescension. Or possibly she correctly perceived that beneath my Brooks Brothers button-down blue oxford shirt, Repp tie and tweedy sports jacket from Bloomingdales, I essentially was a wharf rat from New Bedford, Massachusetts.

Our conversation became very stilted. For some reason or other we were irritating each other. Then she made an unexpected request. She said that she wanted each forthcoming *Sergeant* to contain at least three sex scenes!

That request really pissed me off. How dare this pain in the ass tell me what to write? I replied that *The Sergeant* was about front-line combat, there were no women in the front lines, therefore her request was unrealistic. She became equally pissed off and even more arrogant. We were arguing when Walter returned to the office. His facial expression indicated his disappointing realization that my interaction with the Bantam exec had not gone well. Shortly thereafter I left his office. The Bantam exec probably told Walter that I had been obnoxious.

My first Bantam novel in *The Sergeant* series was #4 *The Liberation of Paris*. I thought it would especially appeal to Walter because he had been a sergeant during World War II and actually participated in the liberation of Paris.

One of the characters in *The Liberation of Paris* happened to be Ernest Hemingway himself with whom Sergeant Mahoney drinks cognac and smokes cigars. I also wrote in Jean-Paul Sartre but an editor removed him for some reason. Many other historical figures also made in person appearances such as Chancellor Adolf Hitler, General Alfred Jodl, and General Dietrich von Choltitz, military governor of Paris whom Hitler had ordered to destroy the city. But Choltitz disobeyed the order at great risk to himself because like most people who've visited the City of Light, he loved Paris.

I wrote five more novels in *The Sergeant* series for a total of nine overall. I regret to report that sales were not nearly as great as Walter predicted. They didn't even come close. To my best recollection, each sold in the 40,000 to 60,000 copies range like most of my other novels. Needless to say, I never bought the black Corvette or other items, and remained in my Hell's Kitchen squalid apartment for many more years.

I never reproached Walter for miscalculating future sales for *The Sergeant*. A writer dare not antagonize his publisher. But I was very disappointed and still am to this day.

All *The Sergeant* novels have been republished as ebooks by Len Levinson.

27

MY GREAT AMERICAN TAXICAB NOVEL

I COMPLETED *CABBY* IN 1972. IT WAS THE SECOND NOVEL that I ever completed but didn't get published until 1980. Supposedly a so-called "serious" novel, it was written before I ever dreamed of becoming an action/adventure razzle-dazzle author.

I actually believed *Cabby* would win widespread critical acclaim, make lots of money, possibly even a movie deal, and establish me as a great American novelist on the level of Saul Bellow, Norman Mailer, John Cheever, Bernard Malamud, John Updike, etc, which proves yet again that self-deception is the primary occupational hazard of writers.

Here's the context for this major delusion:

As explained in Chapter One, I quit my PR job in 1971 to become a writer of novels, most exalted ambition of my life. I had no intention whatever of becoming an action/adventure razzle dazzle novelist. My goal as stated above was to become a great American novelist, but my first so-called "serious" novel took about a year to write and got rejected everywhere. I'll describe it in greater detail later because it was one of the last books of mine to be published.

I was shattered by the rejection of that first novel, then called *Tropical Disturbance*, now called *Cobra Woman*, because I thought it surely would be published by a major hardcover house fairly quickly, another of my self-deceptions. Instead, I was running out of money and needed a part-time job so I could continue writing.

Like many artsy types, I became a cabdriver on the mean streets of New York City. Unfortunately, during the early 1970s an average of four cabdrivers were murdered each month.

Some cabbies drove during the day because they couldn't handle dangers of the night. Others drove during the night because they couldn't manage daytime traffic. I drove on the night shift for the Metropolitan Garage on 11th Avenue and 56th Street in Manhattan's Hell's Kitchen, when I was living downtown in Greenwich Village, which meant a long subway commute in the middle of the night to go home after work.

I drove on Thursday, Friday and Saturday nights. My shifts began at 4pm and ended at 4am. All sorts of people sat in the back seat of my taxicabs, such as secretaries, doctors, Wall Street brokers, prostitutes, construction workers, department store salespersons, cops, criminals, wealthy women going shopping, couples on dates, advertising copywriters, incredibly beautiful women, alcoholics, drug addicts, raving lunatics, people going home to high crime neighborhoods, movie stars Deborah Kerr, Robert Duvall and Elliot Gould, and even my former PR boss Lee Solters got into my cab one night, astonished to see me behind the wheel.

A few male passengers received fellatio in the back seat while I was driving them and their female or male paramours wherever they wanted to go. Occasionally passengers would get out in dangerous neighborhoods without paying because they knew I wouldn't dare follow them.

While driving this zoo of passengers to their destinations, and during long stretches when I was cruising without anyone in the back seat, I felt inspired to write a great American novel about a cabdriver who didn't have all his marbles, who in many ways was me.

So when not driving I sat at home in my Christopher Street tenement pad writing the novel that became *Cabby*. I had virtually no social life during this period and sank into very strange, isolated frames of mind which seeped into the novel.

Finally, I finished *Cabby* and was very pleased with the result, which turned out sort of like James Joyce spiked with Henry Miller with a dollop of Fyodor Dostoesvky on the side. I delivered the manuscript to my then literary agent Elaine Markson whose office was nearby on Greenwich Avenue. Elaine actually liked this peculiar novel and submitted it to major publishers.

An editor at Little, Brown wanted to publish it in hardcover. I don't remember this editor's name; she was Chinese-American in her twenties and took me to lunch at a fancy mid-Manhattan restaurant where she said that she considered *Cabby* outstandingly original.

Everything looked rosy; it appeared that the novel soon would be published by Little, Brown but unfortunately the brass there disagreed with the editor and rejected *Cabby*. Subsequently it was rejected by numerous other publishers.

Meanwhile I desperately wanted to escape cabdriving because I thought, according to the law of averages, I'd probably get killed fairly soon on some dark night in one of New York City's high crime neighborhoods where often I found myself. I wondered if I'd be alive next morning when I rode the subway to the Metropolitan garage each afternoon.

Finally, I hit on an escape strategy. I'd write hardcore erotic novels to earn my daily tofu and quit driving taxicabs. Amazingly, the plan worked. My first and only 100% hardcore erotic novel became *Private Sessions* by March Hastings, which I've described earlier in this book. It was published in 1973 by Midwood, a subsidiary of Belmont Tower, first novel of any kind I'd had published.

That publication led to writing action/adventure novels for BT where my first editor Peter McCurtin taught me essentials of storytelling, emphasizing the all-important technique of narrative tension. Finally, my so-called literary career was launched, and I didn't need to drive a cab anymore. I soon discovered that I actually enjoyed writing action/adventure novels.

I developed such a good relationship with BT that they even published *Cabby* in 1980. I dedicated it to Milburn Smith who succeeded Peter as my editor. Unfortunately, *Cabby* sold very poorly. It was not my great breakthrough novel, not even close.

I hated the cover Belmont-Tower commissioned for *Cabby*. The guy shown driving the cab looked nothing like bearded tormented half-insane Shumsky the cabdriver as I described him in the novel. The cover doesn't in the least capture the dark sinister psychotic mood of the novel. Evidently the artist never read it. *Cabby* needed a cover artist with the skill and sensitivity of a Tony Masero.

In 2014, Joe Kenney asked me to write something about *Cabby* for his *Glorious Trash* blog. I barely remembered the novel so reread it for the first time since around 1979 and soon came to the depressing realization that it wasn't The Great American Taxicab Novel after all, and in fact was seriously flawed.

Cabby isn't really a story. It's mostly a series of cab rides interspersed with episodes in the life of a semi-bonkers cabdriver named Shumsky who'd been traumatized by the break-up of his marriage, as I still was traumatized by the break-up of mine. It has lots of authentic early 1970s color and many interesting scenes but overall didn't have much narrative tension, which detracted from readability.

Cabby was written before the movie *Taxi Driver* starring Robert De Niro was released in 1976, so the movie could not have influenced me. *Cabby* was published in 1980 which meant screenwriter Paul Schrader could not have read it before writing *Taxi Driver*. Yet certain curious similarities can be found between the movie and my novel. It's almost enough to make one believe in Carl Jung's theory of the Collective Unconscious.

There are two hard-core erotic sequences in *Cabby* which I found embarrassing to read 41 years later, although I suppose there's truth in them somewhere. Men really do go crazy over women and have grotesque sexual fantasies. At least I did in those days. Those two sequences were disturbing and even disgusting from my viewpoint at age 79 when I reread the novel. Male sexuality is very different at age 37 compared with age 79. I must have been a very strange dude back in 1972.

Cabby was an attempt by a neophyte to write a complex literary novel influenced by James Joyce, Henry Miller and Fyodor Dostoevsky, but didn't quite succeed I don't think. I can't recommend this novel, but writers aren't always best judges of their work. We can be too critical or not critical enough.

Here are some excerpts from Joe Kenney's review:

If the novel lacks much of a plot or characterization, it more than makes up for it with Len's usual knack for capturing '70s New York. *Cabby* almost acts like a guidebook, with Shumsky detailing which streets he uses to get around Manhattan and environs, telling us of the people and places there. We also get a good cross-section of the type of people who lived in NYC at the time, though [...] our narrator rarely interacts with them."

The biggest difference between *Cabby* and Len's later novels is that here he really brings on the "literary" stuff, with themes and allusions and metaphors weaved into the novel, sometimes overbearingly so, particularly Shumsky's penchant for thinking of himself as a Catholic saint, struggling and toiling for salvation. There are many sequences which almost go into stream-of-consciousness, as Len brings these blood-soaked fantasies to life, with Shumsky seeing Jesus bleeding on the cross in Times Square and etc. It gets to be a bit much at times, however the writing itself is good, and it's interesting to see a different side of Len's style.

Not that there are no flashes of enjoyment in the novel. For one I was happy to see that, even in his first [actually second written] novel, Len was serving up unusual and memorable supporting characters, not to mention his knack for featuring the same characters in different novels; Shumsky at one point is shocked when his old boss from the PR firm gets in his cab, and it's none other than Larry Walters from *Hype!* (And

Shumsky himself made a cameo in *The Bar Studs* – yet
he was more memorable in those few pages than he is in
the entirety of *Cabby*.)

I don't disagree with anything Joe wrote in this
review. He was very insightful as always. Yet I still love
Cabby as an accurate mirror of Manhattan low life in the
early 1970s, and it almost works as a serious hallucina-
tory literary novel influenced by James Joyce, Henry
Miller and Fyodor Dostoyevsky.

Cabby never has been republished in paperback or as
ebooks, which perhaps is a great benefit for world
literature.

28

I AM "THE LAST BUFFOON"

DURING EARLY YEARS OF MY SO-CALLED LITERARY CAREER, as I reflected upon my day-to-day existence, it all seemed rather strange compared to most people with normal jobs and enough income to pay bills.

The more I ruminated on my pulp fiction agony and ecstasy, the more I realized it might provide a framework rich with possibilities for a comic novel in the tradition of other comic novels about mad artists such as *The Ginger Man* by J.P. Donleavy, *The Horse's Mouth* by Joyce Carey, and *The Fan Man* by my old buddy William Kotzwinkle.

I decided to call my mad artist novel *The Last Buffoon*. The title obviously is similar to *The Last Tycoon* by F. Scott Fitzgerald, but plot and characters of *The Last Buffoon* were not at all similar to *The Last Tycoon*. The truth is that I considered myself the real last buffoon because of my seemingly ridiculous lifestyle.

So it came to pass that sometime in the 1970s when I was living in Manhattan, I sat before my IBM Selectric typewriter and began banging out this weird semi-autobiographical tale which became a true psychological portrait of my reality and state of mind during that period when I was immersed most of the time in my literary imagination instead of the real world, writing entire novels in only six weeks, one after the other, living hand to mouth, minimal social life, and my publishers never paid me their paltry sums on time as stipulated in their own contracts. One of my editors, the great Peter McCurtin at Belmont-Tower, told me that if I wanted to get paid, I'd need to break into the office safe!

What kind of demented personality would choose such a stressful, low-income life? The short answer is that I enjoyed writing fiction and hated every job I ever had. It's not like I had better alternatives such as IBM, General Motors or other corporations offering me $100,000 per year to head up their publicity departments. The way I saw it in my hyped-up melodramatic brain, my choice was to become a successful writer or die trying.

These attitudes carried over into *The Last Buffoon*. The protagonist and my alter ego became Alexander Frapkin, a name I considered appropriately pompous and ludicrous for this fictional version of *moi*. Alexander Frapkin was Lenny Levinson exaggerated to the max. All my frustrations, confusions and warped insights were dumped into the novel and spun to make them more bizarre.

The Last Buffoon is not 100% autobiographical. I never masturbated in movie theaters. No Mafia hoodlum ever beat me up because his 15-year-old daughter became corrupted by one of my novels. No one ever hung me out of a window by my heels.

The Last Bufoon's female lead character is an Argentine illegal immigrant named Mabra based on my second wife Alba, an immigrant from Uruguay. I did not marry Alba for cash payment as Frapkin married Mabra. I married Alba because she was a former girlfriend and I felt sorry for her; I didn't want her to get deported. And Alba showed her deep appreciation, respect, love and devotion by doing her best to drive me out of my mind, as did Mabra to Frapkin in the novel.

I completed the manuscript in around six months, as I recall. My then literary agent, the magnificent Elaine Markson, was enthusiastic about it but unable to close a sale. Many years later I convinced my new editor at Belmont-Tower, Milburn Smith, to publish it. For the cover he used a photo of me standing in a trash barrel in Washington Square Park in Greenwich Village. The photo was snapped by another old buddy, Seymour Linden, a professional photographer who worked for a photo agency named Black Star that sent him all over the world to cover riots, revolutions and wars. Regarding the trash barrel in the photo, it probably was where I belonged.

I am not wearing a costume in the cover photo. I actually walked around NYC in that outfit. I looked exactly like the madman that I was in those days. I probably frightened little children and elderly ladies. *The Last Buffoon* was published in 1980 under my pseudonym Leonard Jordan.

I hated the jacket copy: "The hilarious novel that proves all the world loves a loser!" Who wants to read about a loser, no matter how hilarious he might be? Losers are depressing. The copywriter should have sold the novel as a nutty comic masterpiece. Frapkin viewed himself not as a loser but soon-to-be-winner. In a larger sense, he was just another struggling New York writer with delusions of grandeur and tendencies to get into jams.

After publication in 1980 I received more fan mail for *The Last Buffoon* than any of my other novels. Two options for movies were contracted but no movie ever was made. Around 2010 a Los Angeles screenwriter optioned the novel for a third time. He promised to write a great screenplay, claimed to know many important movers and shakers in the film industry, thought he could convince Sasha Baron Cohen to play Frapkin, but for some reason this screenwriter never wrote a screenplay and suddenly stopped communicating with me. To this day I don't understand his game. Perhaps he died?

Joe Kenney reviewed *The Last Buffoon* for his *Glorious Trash* blog. Below are a few of his comments:

> Back in 2005 I discovered this paperback original in a used bookstore -- a signed copy, at that. Only, it was signed "Leonard Levinson." This confused me at the time, given that the book was credited to Leonard Jordan. It was only later that I discovered that "Jordan" was a pseudonym of prolific writer Leonard Levinson, who among many, many other novels cranked out a few volumes of the always-entertaining *Sharpshooter* series.
>
> When I first read the novel a few years ago I really enjoyed it; upon this re-reading, I loved it. Simply put, anyone who enjoys the men's adventure genre or the trashy paperback fiction of the 1970s must read this novel. Especially if like me you've often wondered, Who the hell writes this sort of trash? Levinson offers a first-rate glimpse into the zany life of a paperback writer living in the slummy New York City of the late 1970s.
>
> For me one of Levinson's greatest strengths is his ability to bring to life any character, no matter how

minor. Characters in his novels always jump off the page and The Last Buffoon is no exception. It's like all of his characters have lives outside of the book and are just making guest appearances.

Perhaps the most enjoyable element though is how The Last Buffoon shows the mind of a writer at work.

Finally, the novel offers a great view of late 1970s New York City, a long-gone sleazepit of 42nd Street porno theaters and rampant crime. Again, this book's highly recommended for connoisseurs of trash fiction and men's adventure novels, particularly the more lurid 1970s incarnation of the genre. It's a lot of fun, moves at a snappy pace, and it's well written to boot. In a way The Last Buffoon reminds me of William Kotzwinkle's The Fan Man in that both novels are about eternal optimists who are even more crazy than the crazy characters they meet. But whereas The Fan Man attained a sort of cult fame, The Last Buffoon went unnoticed, and that's a shame.

Now back to me, Lenny Levinson. Yes, it's a shame I never became a rich famous writer, never enjoyed love affairs with gorgeous movie stars like Raquel Welch, Ali McGraw and Faye Dunaway, never resided in a penthouse on Central Park South, never vacationed on the French Riviera. But I absolutely loved writing The Last Buffoon and have no regrets at all. It was a wonderful cathartic creative adventure. Many times I laughed out loud at scenes I was creating. I felt very inspired while writing this novel.

Recently I re-read The Last Bufoon. What a strange story. The vulgarity is way over the top. It doesn't fit into any category. What kind of degenerated mind could conceive such an extravagantly bizarre novel?

Evidently the kind of degenerated mind that believed in his vision of himself as a great writer. I can't explain why I held so tightly to this belief. It was sort of like religion. I felt absolutely certain that one day soon I'd advance to the level of Norman Mailer, John Cheever, John Updike, Philip Roth, Saul Bellow, etc.

Obviously, I was deluded. I now believe that becoming a successful author is like winning the lottery. All odds were stacked high against me, but I gave my literary career the best of my intelligence, such as it was, and my spirit, if it exists, and my overloaded imagination, for all the good it did me, and now despite everything I'm finally at peace with myself and the world at age 85.

THE LAST BUFFOON has been republished under my real name in paperback and ebooks targeted at possible readers who might feel curious or sufficiently emboldened to take a deep dive into the bizarre life of a pulp fiction author/buffoon.

29

MY GREAT AMERICAN NAZI
NOVEL

I WAS BORN IN MASSACHUSETTS 1935. MY consciousness formed during the era when Nazis were much in the news. Comic books that I read were full of wicked Nazis. I became fascinated by Hitler and the Nazis who seemed to represent pure evil of unbelievable proportions, yet Nazis were all too real, not simply comic book characters.

My fascination with Nazis continues to this day. How could human beings behave with such cruelty toward other human beings? How could the nation that produced Beethoven, Kant and Thomas Mann also raise Hitler to power? What was happening inside the heads of Nazi fanatics and ordinary people who supported them?

In an effort to understand, I read a tremendous amount of books about Nazis, as well as writings and speeches by Hitler and other leading Nazis. To this day I continue reading about Nazis, recently completing the second volume of a new two-volume bio of *Hitler* by

Volker Ullrich, which I recommend without reservations.

When I became a writer, I wanted to write a novel about Nazis in the spy thriller mode popularized by John Le Carré, Robert Ludlum, Ken Follett, Hammond Innes, Eric Ambler, Jack Higgins, Alistair MacLean, and Frederick Forsyth, among others. I thought such a novel would allow me to plumb the depths of the Nazi psyche, and possibly become a best-seller.

Where should I begin my Nazi novel? What could the plot be? Who might be the characters? I could have gone in innumerable directions but finally decided to focus on what might have happened beneath the surface during the final months of World War Two in Europe and shortly thereafter, told from the viewpoint of research filtered through my idiosyncratic brain.

One of the most fascinating Nazis was Hermann Goering who had been a fighter pilot during World War One, eventually becoming commander of the famed Richthofen Squadron and winning the Pour Le Merité, Germany's highest award for valor, similar to the American Congressional Medal of Honor or Britain's Victoria Cross.

He was not extremely anti-Semitic like Hitler, Himmler and Goebbels, but joined the National Socialist German Workers Party (Nazis) after World War One because he was a nationalist dissatisfied with what he considered the Weimar government's incompetence, and what he considered injustices of the Versailles Treaty. Like many others, he fell under the oratory spell of Adolf Hitler.

Goering participated in the Beer Hall Putsch of 1923, got shot in the groin, was treated with painkillers, and as a result became a drug addict until surrendering to the American Army at the end of World War Two.

I doubt that anyone could join the Nazis without being anti-Semitic to a greater or lesser degree, because Jew hatred was the primary philosophy of Hitler. According to Roger Manvell and Heinrich Fraenkel, who wrote an excellent biography of Goering: "Goering was not anti-Jewish from emotional needs; he became anti-Jewish because the party policy required him to do so. If he liked a man enough he was quite prepared to overlook the Jewish blood in his veins."

Goering said: "I will decide who is a Jew."

After becoming a morphine addict, Goering grew obese and weird, wearing peculiar costumes and garish cosmetics at home. Some thought him charming and intelligent, but he was brutal to his enemies. There is no doubt that he was up to his eyeballs in slave labor policies of the Third Reich but had no involvement in death camps according to historians. It is generally believed that heavy duty drugs probably unbalanced his mind.

Goering became second to Hitler in the Nazi hierarchy and used his power to collect a huge trove of art, gold and jewels. When planning my Nazi novel, I wondered whatever happened to all that swag. It seemed obvious that many people and organizations must have wanted it, including diehard Nazis, ordinary German criminals and the American Army.

That became my plot: various groups trying to acquire or steal the famed Goering Treasure in final tumultuous months of war and its aftermath. While writing *The Goering Treasure*, I tried to show the vast panorama of German society when the Third Reich was going down the tubes. Many historical characters appear in the novel, including Goering himself plus Joseph

Goebbels, Martin Bormann, Eva Braun and even Adolph Hitler making several in-person appearances.

One of the most vicious, horrifying scenes that I ever wrote appeared in the original paperback version. It was so over the top unbelievable that I rewrote it for the novel's republication.

The Goering Treasure by pseudonym Gordon Davis was published originally by Zebra in 1980. I reread it recently and had to admit that it was not very similar to the works of Ludlum, Follett, Forsyth and the others, although it had much drama, irony and many action/adventure qualities.

I've learned during my long literary career that I cannot write like anyone else. I can only write like me, for better or worse, although I certainly have been influenced by many other writers.

The Goering Treasure provided a vast canvas on which my lurid imagination ran wild. After completion I thought it absolutely brilliant.

Unfortunately, the book-buying public did not agree. *The Goering Treasure* did not become a bestseller as I'd hoped, or even come close, although Zebra gave it what I considered a great cover. *C'est la vie*, man.

30

MY FIRST SUBMARINE NOVEL

ONE DAY CIRCA 1979 I WAS SITTING IN THE EAST 50S office of paperback packager Jim Bryans whom I've mentioned before in connection with *The Sergeant* series.

Jim said that he wanted me to write two novels in a World War II submarine series he had created called *The Silent Service*. He said that no book with a submarine on the cover ever lost money.

I probably signed the contract then and there. Jim said I'd write the first book in the series, so presumably he had confidence that I could launch it in grand style. I had the same confidence. He would pay more than I usually received for writing novels, so I quickly became enthusiastic about the project.

Jim asked if I knew anything about submarines. I told him I'd read a few World War II submarine books and watched a few World War II submarine movies. He suggested that I tour an American World War II submarine and German U-Boat at a U.S. Navy installation in Groton, Connecticut, accompanied by another writer on the series, John van Zweinen who also was technical advisor for the series.

One morning shortly thereafter I rode a commuter train to the Connecticut town where John van Zweinen lived. He was waiting for me at the station, around six feet six inches tall like Jim, lean and rangy, short beard, wearing a Greek-style sailors cap, probably in his 50s like Jim.

His car was a sleek BMW. While driving he told me he had been a paperback book cover artist and recently turned to writing novels. Finally we arrived at the site of two vintage submarines floating near each other and tethered to the shore of the Thames River.

First we explored the American submarine, small and cramped inside, gray-painted metallic walls covered with pipes, dials, levers, switches, wheels, other controls, a periscope in the conning tower. The lighting was dim; I felt claustrophobic and wondered how men could live for long periods in such spartan confined space, stinky due to rudimentary bathing facilities, knowing they could be blown to bits by depth charges, bombed by aircraft when on the surface, or shelled by enemy ships.

The German U-boat was even smaller and more cramped but otherwise similar. Both subs were lethal underwater killing machines, no luxury or comfort allowed.

After our submarine tour John dropped me off at the rail station, and I rode a commuter train back to NYC. My next step was to buy or check out of the library a substantial number of books about submarines during World War II. My favorite was *Das Boot (The Boat)* by Lothar Günthar Buchheim, a photographer on German subs during World War II, who had been depth charged numerous times. I also watched the German movie based on the book and thought it outstanding.

One of the most important and useful books that I read was *The Battle Of The Atlantic* by Terry Hughes and John Costello. I also read a non-fiction book about the sinking of the submarine *USS Squalus*, the incident that was the basis for the fictionalized plot I was supposed to write. The title of my first submarine novel would be *Forty Fathoms Down* by J. Farragut Jones, the pseudonym used by all authors hired to work on the submarine series.

I was on deadline so couldn't continue reading and watching movies indefinitely. Finally, I needed to sit and write. Jim had given me a two-page typewritten description of the series concept which included the first novel's basic plot and list of characters to appear in all novels. It was up to me to knit everything together into a coherent story with word count of 90,000 compared to around 60,000 words for most novels I'd written under contract thus far.

Jim's plot outline was based on the true incident mentioned above, the sinking of the new *USS Squalus*, a Sargo class submarine that inadvertently dropped to the bottom on its 19th test dive off the coast of Portsmouth, New Hampshire on 23 May 1939. Failure of the main induction valve caused flooding of the aft torpedo room, both engine rooms and the crew's quarters, drowning 26 men quickly and initiating a much-publicized massive rescue operation for 33 survivors in sealed chambers of the stricken submarine, their oxygen diminishing every minute.

This certainly was a dramatic premise but offered no opportunity for war action although I'd thought *The Silent Service* was about submarine warfare. Lacking naval battles to provide conflict and narrative tension, I needed to invent conflict among crew members of the sunken submarine as well as conflict among members of the research effort, with romantic complications concerning women connected to officers and enlisted sailors involved in the suspenseful melodrama.

Now I come to a very troubling incident which I feel compelled to mention in the spirit of full disclosure. I really shouldn't touch it with a ten-foot pole but often I've had extraordinarily poor judgement and this probably is another example. The most terrible scene I ever wrote was written into this novel. I feel humiliated to this day because it makes me appear antisemitic although I'm Jewish myself.

Here's how it happened: One of the main characters conceived by Jim was Jewish naval officer Lieutenant Commander Ben Mount, probably based on a younger version of Admiral Hyman G. Rickover (1900-1986) who led the project to develop atomic submarines and was said to be abrasive at times.

I wondered how to present this Jewish Lieutenant Commander Ben Mount objectively and make him an interesting character. I definitely didn't want him to be some kind of SuperJew astonishingly intelligent, incredibly heroic, the pinnacle of virtue and a beacon of light for the ages, but also definitely didn't want a seagoing Woody Allen nudnik, nebbish or schlemiel.

Then I remembered a distant cousin around 20 years older than I. Everyone in the family called him Tutti. He was the first Jew from my hometown of New Bedford, Massachusetts to graduate from the U.S. Naval Academy at Annapolis. He served around eight years on active duty, then resigned his commission to become a corporate executive.

Tutti's father was a plumber who owned his own small plumbing business and spent most of his professional life crawling around flooded basements, or fixing toilets and faucets, or installing pipes and plumbing gadgets, which means Tutti was not exactly from a distinguished background like many Naval officers in those days from upper class Anglo-Saxon Protestant families.

I'd only been around Tutti a few times. He was tall, built like a professional football fullback, probably worked out in a gym, short black hair parted on the side, good-looking, always seemed steady, rational and deliberate. I decided that Tutti would be the ideal model for Lieutenant Commander Ben Mount.

While trying to construct his character, I naturally wondered what could be going on inside the head of a Jewish naval officer from a plumbing family who worked with other officers from patrician Anglo-Saxon Protestant backgrounds.

The psychology of characters always has been important to me because a reader cannot connect with a novel unless characters are compelling. I try to avoid straightforward descriptions of characters' psychologies, preferring instead to stage scenes revealing their inner lives in action. It was with highest artistic literary intentions I wrote the sequence that now sickens me even to think about.

Ben was home on furlough, seated at a dinner table with several members of his extended family who happened to be loud, ill-mannered, obnoxious, sloppy in their eating habits, and Ben couldn't help comparing them with his elegant upper class fellow officers and their families. I was trying to show the disturbing dichotomy between his old plumbing family background and present reality as naval officer, but the scene became too contrived, exaggerated, disconnected with reality, and seemed like the author was putting down Jews.

I never have dined with Jewish adults or any other adults who behaved as badly as my fabricated Jews in that scene. I don't know where its extreme hyperbolic overkill came from and didn't realize how off base I was until the novel was printed and I read the scene with mounting horror. Joseph Goebbels would have loved the scene. It was like articles printed in *Der Sturmer*.

From the perspective of today, I can guess more or less what went wrong. I was writing quickly to complete the novel on time, not paying sufficient attention to what was happening in sentences describing this critical scene. I just dashed it off without deeper reflection on a situation requiring utmost delicacy and stone-cold honesty. If I'd given the scene more thought, I would have written it more intelligently and with much more punch than this over-the-top antisemitic horror show.

Forty Fathoms Down was not a big bestseller which means not many people read it, thank goodness. It goes to show what can happen when a writer loses perspective and becomes careless. How could I concoct such a scene? What in the hell was wrong with me? Why didn't Jim force me to rewrite the scene?

Jim called a few weeks after I delivered the manuscript. He said that *Forty Fathoms Down* would be second in the series, not first as originally planned. He had decided that for maximum impact his submarine saga should begin with a war action novel.

P.S. *Forty Fathoms Down* has been republished under my real name in paperback and as ebooks. I have rewritten the offensive scene which now does what I wanted. Now it has punch.

31

MY SECOND SUBMARINE NOVEL

My SECOND SUBMARINE NOVEL THAT I WROTE FOR paperback packager Jim Bryans is one of my favorite novels that I ever wrote out of 86 published.

It was #5 in *The Silent Service* series by J. Farragut Jones, published by Jim and Dell in 1981. I also wrote #2 *Forty Fathoms Down* which I've described above.

As with #2, Jim gave me a two-page outline describing overall plot and continuing characters. *Tracking The Wolf Pack* covered the most critical period in the battle for the North Atlantic during World War II, providing plenty of opportunity to write naval war action and associated dramatic plot elements.

I wanted to tell this story from both American and German points of view, with characters of all kinds from fanatical Nazis to professional patriotic German officers, from ordinary American and British sailors to highest ranking officers in the Allied navies. I also wanted interesting women because men and women tend to get crazy over each other under normal circumstances, but emotions become especially intense during wartime.

I couldn't write off the top of my head a 90,000-word novel about a specific period in history requiring extensive knowledge of complex technologies related to submarines and anti-submarine warfare. A tremendous amount of research was required. I read the below books which still are in my home library:

Memoirs: Ten Years And Twenty Days by Admiral Karl Dönitz, commander of the German U-Boat fleet

Convoy by Martin Middlebrook, about the "Greatest Convoy Battle Of All Time", said to be a turning point in the Battle of the Atlantic

Iron Coffins: A Personal Account Of The German U-Boat Battles Of World War II by Herbert A. Werner, former U-boat commander

Jane's Pocket Book Of Submarine Development edited by John Moore

The Bluejacket's Manual 1943

The Battle Of The Atlantic: The First Complete Account Of The Origins And Outcome Of The Longest And Most Crucial Campaign Of World War Ii by Terry Hughes and John Costello

Submarine Commander by Rear Admiral Ben Bryant

U-Boat Killer by Captain Donald MacIntyre

Escort Commander: The Story Of Captain Frederic John Walker by Terence Robertson

Das Boot (The Boat) a novel by Lothar-Günther Buchheim who had served aboard U-boats.

U-Boat War, by Lothar-Günther Buchheim

How To Abandon Ship by Phil Richards & John J. Banigan, published in 1942 when such a book was necessary.

I also read many other books and watched several

World War II submarine movies. I even toured and took notes aboard two vintage World War II submarines at a U.S. Navy installation in Groton, Connecticut, which I mentioned previously. The American submarine was the *U.S.S. Croaker* but I don't remember nomenclature of the German U-boat.

The danger of research is that a writer can be tempted to stuff it all into the novel to show how thorough he has been. But tons of research can sink a novel with extraneous details. A writer must use research selectively because narrative tension is the primary goal of storytelling, in my opinion. The most important benefit of wide-ranging research is that a writer can feel confident about not making egregious mistakes.

The concept of the wolf pack was developed by German Admiral Karl Dönitz during World War One when he was a young naval officer in a British prisoner of war camp. He reasoned that groups of submarines acting in concert, directed by radio from headquarters, utilizing latest intelligence about enemy shipping, would be more effective than individual submarines cruising about randomly, searching for targets.

Research plunged my mind deeply into submarine warfare. I have a very vivid imagination and often felt panic and claustrophobia when reading about U-boats getting depth-charged, or the thrill of the hunt as British ships chased and depth-charged U-boats.

Tracking The Wolf Pack covers a period beginning with U-boat wolf packs attacking Allied convoys almost with impunity, then to evolution of Allied tactics and technology that could locate and destroy U-boats, and finally to increasing destruction of the U-boat fleet.

The first paragraph of the novel is reproduced verbatim here:

> It was night in the middle of the Atlantic Ocean.
> Kapitänlieutnant Joachim Kruger stood on the bridge of
> U-112 and studied the British convoy through his
> binoculars. The U-boat was pointed in a north-westerly
> direction, and the convoy was headed east toward the
> British Isles. There was no moon and Kruger had his U-
> boat trimmed low in the water.

Now back to this article. Kruger and the rest of the
U-boat wolf pack attack the convoy. Ships are blown up,
flaming oil covers the water, and many sailors are
burned alive or drowned in a brutal scene not
uncommon in the crucial battle for the North Atlantic.
Meanwhile the convoy's escort ships search desperately
through smoke and oil slick flames for U-boats. Many of
the novel's main characters are introduced in these sea
battle scenes.

I prefer to start novels with action instead of exposition. Action reveals character and propels the narrative
from the get-go. A story must move, not lay dead in the
water.

Hitler had conquered most of Europe by the time the
novel begins. Virtually all of Great Britain's supplies
came via ships from the United States. Hitler needed to
stop those ships. The Allies needed them to get through.
This is the grim tension that fuels *Tracking The Wolf Pack*.
You can't get more dramatic than that.

During the course of the war, 2,572 Allied merchant
and war ships were sunk by U-boats, and 1,133 U-boats
were sunk by Allied war ships according to *The Battle Of
The Atlantic* mentioned above.

Making in-person appearances in the novel are none
other than rapidly aging and increasingly delusional
Adolf Hitler himself; Grand Admiral Karl Dönitz,

commander of the U-Boat fleet; Admiral Percy Noble, Commander of the Western Approaches for Great Britain; plus several other real life individuals or characters based on real life individuals.

The 90,000-word requirement offered a more expansive playing field and more opportunity for adding depth to the plot, and for contriving subplots feeding into the main plot, making it more complex, interesting and involving for the reader (and me), but at the same I could not allow additional space to entice me into becoming sloppy or allowing the story to become slack and boring.

So the big question is: Did all my research, plans and intellectualizing actually produce something worthwhile? I read *Tracking The Wolf Pack* a few years ago and considered it surprisingly good if not almost excellent, considering I wrote it in only two months. Somehow I achieved my ambitions for this particular story except for a few brief instances of vulgarity which dragged down into the sewer an otherwise compelling narrative.

Tracking The Wolf Pack has been republished under my real name in paperback and as ebooks.

This was my last submarine novel for Jim Bryans but we weren't finished with each other yet. He would ask me to write more novels which will be described in due course.

32

MY GREAT AMERICAN SLEAZY
TIMES SQUARE NOVEL

DURING THE LATE 1970s, I LIVED IN A STUDIO APARTMENT on West 55th Street between 8th and 9th Avenues, not far from Times Square when it was the porn capitol of America, loaded with peep shows, porn movie theaters, massage parlors, porn bookstores, prostitution, and every kind of sexual vice imaginable.

Often I walked through the area on my way to the library at 42nd and 5th, or to a certain health food store near the library, or to Macy's on 34th Street, or other destinations. As a social science major in college, and amateur sex maniac in private life, I soon found myself wandering into various Times Square establishments to see what was going on. Becoming increasingly intrigued, I started prowling Times Square at night when the action really was happening.

Fortunately or unfortunately, I was and remain a romantic who believed then and now in true love until the end of time, despite all evidence to the contrary. With this mindset, I didn't consider Times Square very erotic, although it disturbed me quite a lot.

The women who performed in live sex shows seemed pathetic. The lonely, desperate men who drooled over them seemed even more pathetic. The aura of sexual sickness depressed me but also was fascinating because it represented the human psyche in its most freaky modality.

Times Square in that era offered a degraded form of eros because you had to pay for sex, whether looking at a peep show, sitting in a porn movie house, buying a porn magazine, or getting laid in a massage parlor with a drugged out, mentally disturbed, not very attractive woman, probably somebody's mother or even grandmother. Times Square successfully separated sex from love, turning me off and turning me on at the same time.

It wasn't long before a story and characters started forming in my overheated imagination. I'm not the kind of writer who sits down and willfully concocts a plot. Instead, I see a movie in my mind and write it down. It's more about inspiration than intention.

The protagonist detective Danny Rackman was me in the guise of a cop. His girlfriend, Francie, was based on a woman I was involved with at the time. And the serial killer was based on an acquaintance of mine, a very angry man whom I believed capable of murder. But from another perspective, the serial killer also was me.

Nietzsche once said that when you look deeply into evil, then evil also looks deeply into you. I looked deeply into evil when I was writing *Without Mercy* and became scared by what I found inside my mind. I don't claim to be a great writer, but don't like to make superficial characters. So I excavated that killer's head, and it's not a pretty picture.

When Truman Capote wrote about killers in *In Cold Blood*, he presented them very sympathetically as poor lost guys who went wrong. My killer was not a poor lost guy who went wrong. He was very disturbed, angry, and violent, a bad guy whom nobody ever loved. Then one night everything got too much, and he went berserk.

My title was *The Massage Parlor Murders* but the publisher, Zebra Books, changed it to *Without Mercy*, which I'm not sure was an improvement. I read it recently for the first time in around 30 years and found some of my usual maladroit sentences and examples of dubious logic, but the narrative tension and momentum still were working, at least for me.

The story still seemed very real, because as mentioned above, I actually spent many nights investigating the Times Square porn industry, while trying to understand my own sexual needs and occasional anger toward women who didn't always give me what I wanted. It was a journey of self-discovery in addition to a novel I was writing for publication.

I didn't realize it at the time, but I was describing in detail a world that soon would vanish. Amazingly, several years into the future, Times Square would become a branch of Disney World and Toys "R" Us. The bleary-eyed, drugged out whores and pimps evidently transferred their activities elsewhere. I assume they're still in business in somebody else's neighborhood, because as long as there are lonely desperate men, there will be bleary-eyed, drugged out whores and pimps groping for their money.

33

THE MAD ARTIST

As I LOOK BACK AT MY LITERARY CAREER, I THINK I OFTEN appeared to be a mad artist, because I spent most of my days writing novels, which meant sitting alone and opening ponderous doors to my deeper mind which allowed powerful subterranean elements to bubble up.

This opening up process became habitual and after a while I found it extremely difficult to quickly close those ponderous doors in social situations, which meant I often made impulsive statements, or engaged in emotional behavior not socially appropriate, or made too many irrational decisions. I probably appeared mentally unbalanced at times. Perhaps I really was mentally unbalanced at times.

Throughout my life I felt most authentically myself when alone, but in public felt compelled to be charming, amusing and entertaining. This persona came naturally to me. It was not a fake. I loved to make people laugh. I simply could not sit quietly like an inanimate object when in public. I had to become a social animal and contribute to conversations as best I could.

Sometimes I made comments that were funny and caused people to laugh, but unfortunately other times I made comments that were stupid, insulting, vulgar and/or inappropriate because I could not control elements erupting from deepest strata of my mind. I think this opening-up aspect of the creative process helps explain why many artist types appear to be maniacs. We are in touch with intense forces that completely overwhelm us at times.

They certainly overwhelmed me at times, too many times in fact, and still do. This is another of the occupational hazards of being a writer or any other type of artist.

34

MY GREAT AMERICAN WORLD
WAR ONE EPIC NOVEL

AROUND 1980 OR 1981, PAPERBACK PACKAGER JIM Bryans asked me to write a World War One land battle novel for his series *Freedom Fighters* by Jonathan Scofield, to be published by Dell/Bryans.

This ambitious project was a generational saga about several families from upper-, middle- and lower-class backgrounds serving in all of America's wars beginning with the French and Indian War and continuing to Vietnam for a total of 15 novels.

Jim gave me a two-page outline of the World War One novel's basic time frame, plot and characters. It would be called *Bayonets in No-Man's Land* and eventually published in 1983 as #11 in the series.

Jim's outline didn't go into much detail. I'd need to invent around 98% of the story. The contract stipulated 90,000 words.

I felt very excited and highly motivated to write this novel because my father had been a World War One combat veteran and had filled my youthful imagination with wild tales of his experiences. He had served in the famed Second Division and been awarded a ribbon showing six stars representing his participation in six major battle engagements.

The commander of the Second Division had been Major General John A. Lejeune who during World War One gave a speech in which he proclaimed:

"To be able to say, when this war is finished, 'I belonged to the Second Division, and I fought with it at the Battle of Blanc Mont Ridge,' will be the highest honor than can come to any man."

The Battle of Blanc Mont Ridge had been one engagement during the Battle of the Argonne Forest also known as the Meuse/Argonne campaign, for which my father had been awarded one of his battle stars. So evidently my father had been there and earned the highest honor that can come to any man. As a child I idolized the old soldier and viewed him as a great war hero, although he was a nasty son-of-a-bitch at times, and we didn't get along so well when I was a teenager.

Partially influenced by him, but mostly because I wanted the G.I. Bill for college, I enlisted in the Army in 1954 when I was 19, during the Cold War. I served with the 71st and 4th Divisions, not the 2nd like my father. My three years in the Infantry and Corps of Engineers taught me about basic military life up close and personal which meant I could write about it from firsthand experience, although admittedly never was in a hot shooting war.

My Army background combined with tales from my father made me optimistic about writing my World War One novel. I couldn't wait to get started but first needed much research to make sure I didn't screw anything up. So I read many histories of the war plus accounts of individual battles, including biographies and autobiographies of main players, and memoirs of soldiers who'd experienced frontline combat. I wanted to continue reading more and more because World War One was interesting, but I was on deadline and finally had to sit down and write.

Bayonets in No-Man's Land begins on July 4, 1917 when newly arrived doughboys march through the streets of Paris, cheered by massive crowds who hoped the young soldiers would win the war for them. Both French and British armies had been bled white and were exhausted after three years of trench warfare.

The doughboy's commander was Major General John "Blackjack" Pershing who on that day gave a speech at a podium beside the tomb of Marquis de Lafayette, who had fought for America in the Revolutionary War. Blackjack exclaimed in his ringing parade ground voice the famous words: "Lafayette – we are here!"

Many of the novel's main characters are present in this opening sequence including Private Sam Bell based loosely on my father Private Sam Levinson, who told me he also was standing in the ranks on that auspicious day in history.

In addition to General Pershing, the novel also includes other real historical characters such as Captain George Patton, Major George Marshall, Captain Eddie Rickenbacker, Major General LeJeune mentioned above, General Ferdinand Foch, Field Marshal Joseph Joffre, Kaiser Wilhelm II, Field Marshall Paul von Hindenburg, General Erich Ludendorff, Captain Hermann Goering, and young intensely patriotic Private Adolf Hitler, a front-line messenger in the List Regiment.

The situation on the Western Front was dire as the novel opens. The Russian Revolution was building to a climax, and everyone expected Russia to drop out of the war soon, which means the German Army deployed on the Russian front would be redeployed to the Western front where they'd join German troops already there and overwhelm depleted French and British Armies. It was widely believed that only America's doughboys could save Europe from the Kaiser's army.

The doughboys were a big question mark. Could these barely trained American farm and city kids defeat the most formidable war machine in the world? The doughboys were sent to the front after the parade mentioned above. They dug in and waited for the expected major German offensive which soon came with massive unrelenting ferocity.

I wrote about World War One land combat as it was according to history, consisting of tremendous artillery shelling, mass attacks against withering rifle and machine gun fire, brutal bayonet fighting in trenches, poison gas attacks, plus the air war where pilots jousted as in medieval times, riding in airplanes instead of on horses.

Occasionally soldiers and especially pilots spent time in the rear, so naturally there are love affairs in the novel, but I'm pleased to report these interludes are described without pornography that was a hallmark of my earlier novels. *Bayonets in No-Man's Land* was one of the first turning points against my tendencies to get raunchy when describing romance between men and women. I guess I finally was growing up when in my 40s.

I re-read *Bayonets In No-Man's Land* last week for the first time in 15 years or more and considered it quite good considering I wrote it in around two months. I had almost completely forgotten the novel. Many scenes and lines were so wonderful I couldn't believe I wrote them.

The narrative moves along smoothly and held my interest all the way through.

Bayonets in No-Man's Land might have been more successful if published in hardcover as a standalone novel, and promoted with ads in major publications like the New York Times Book Review, but instead the novel received no promotion, publicity or advertising that I ever saw in consumer media, and was #11 in a series where earlier novels by other writers might not have been so wonderful, which would affect sales of later novels like mine.

If I had become a best-selling author early in my literary career, I never would have dreamed of writing a complicated sprawling World War One epic novel. But a desperate pulp fiction writer had to write whatever publishers wanted, which actually was an unexpected benefit because it forced me to research engrossing subjects like World War One, and required me to expand my imagination into areas where I never would have gone if I were a wealthy, successful writer like Norman Mailer, John Cheever, John Updike, Saul Bellow, etc.

Bayonets in No-Man's Land has been republished under my real name as ebooks and in paperback.

35

MY GREAT AMERICAN
AVIATION NOVEL

WHEN I STARTED WRITING NOVELS, IF SOMEONE PREDICTED that someday I'd write one about American aviation in the 1930s, I would have said: "I don't know anything about aviation, am not particularly interested in aviation and have many more important themes that I want to deal with, such as my innumerable demons."

Then in 1982 paperback packager Jim Bryans asked me to write an aviation novel for his *Skymasters* series by Richard Hale Curtis, published by Dell/Bryans. The series consisted of ten novels beginning with earliest days of aviation in America and continuing to modern times.

Skymasters essentially was a generational saga about two families involved in aircraft design, development and production during that long period of world history. I can't be more specific because I never read titles other than mine.

I received a larger advance for my aviation novel than any of my other 86 published novels. The contract stipulated 90,000 words. My contribution became *Every Man An Eagle* #8 in the series.

Jim gave me a two-page outline of plot and main characters. The story, set in the 1930s, is about a ruthless businessman based loosely on Howard Hughes who, by any unscrupulous means, tries to take over an airplane construction company owned by some of the main characters. The story also is about beginnings of commercial passenger aviation, including technological obstacles to be overcome, set against a backdrop of gathering storm clouds leading to World War Two.

I didn't know much about aviation so had to do a lot of reading. My research was extensive, absorbing and opened up an entire world that I hadn't known about before. Aviation is fascinating to read about, but I don't like to fly and always have felt anxious whenever flying.

Finally I banged out the novel, which included lots of Len Levinson trademark conflict, treachery, betrayal and romance, not to mention a full complement of his innumerable demons. I submitted it to Jim and never heard another word about it again. The novel was published by Dell/Bryans in 1983. I didn't read the final printed version until approximately 37 years later.

I expected *Every Man An Eagle* to be very readable, because my other novels for Jim were very readable. I had completely forgotten almost everything about this particular novel so it seemed almost 100% new to me after all these years.

I'm very critical of novels, movies, music, paintings, and art in general, especially my own novels because art and especially my novels cannot improve and possibly become great without rigorous criticism.

While reading *Every Man An Eagle*, I soon encountered problems. The first concerned characters. Several were introduced at the beginning, but the author didn't differentiate them sufficiently. He should have added little details like dirty or manicured fingernails, a wart on a nose, tobacco-stained teeth, a scar on a cheek, ferocious halitosis, nervous tics, sly eyes, cheap suit, his face was long like a sheep's, her movements were graceful as a ballerina, etc. Characters actually became more differentiated as the novel progressed but the author should have done more at the beginning.

The novel's biggest problem was too much stage business cropping up occasionally. By that I mean too many descriptions of people walking or driving from here to there, or lighting or stubbing out cigarettes, or picking up things like telephones or putting them down, or getting dressed or undressed, or excessive descriptions of scenery, or extended sequences of people ruminating about the same concerns over and over, etc. In other words, this novel is not always lean and mean as I like novels to be.

My old friend Bill Kotzwinkle, author of *E.T. The Extra-Terrestrial*, *The Fan Man*, *Hermes 3000*, and numerous other wonderful novels gave me some advice once, while critiquing something I'd written. He said, "Fiction isn't a movie. You needn't show every movement and twitch. Fiction is the realm of inner mind, the second level of reflection."

On another occasion Bill said, "The reader's mind is free fluid, hardly bound at all, and we must appeal to its great mercurial flow, not holding it back with our dull steps."

I encountered too many dull steps and excessive stage business in *Every Man an Eagle*. They are traps into which many writers fall, especially when writing a 90,000-word novel on deadline, but also can be found in novels by successful authors. For example, Lee Childs's novel *Blue Moon* has extended sequences of meaningless stage business, in my opinion. He can get away with it because he's a best-selling author, but Lenny Levinson cannot permit himself the literary indulgence of excessive stage business.

Every Man An Eagle really isn't that flawed, in my admittedly biased opinion. It just has a few problems here and there. The same is true of all novels, to greater or lesser extent. There is no such thing as a perfect novel, but this truism never should become an excuse for sloppy writing.

In the immortal words of one of my favorite all-time authors, the very great William Somerset Maugham: "There are three rules for writing novels. Unfortunately no one knows what they are."

On the plus side, the author of *Every Man An Eagle* developed numerous interesting and fairly original conflicts and subplots. Characters became multi-dimensional after a while and displayed lots of neurotic complications as real people inevitably do. The overarching plot and various subplots work. The author seems to know a lot about aviation and world history in the 1930s but doesn't show off his vast research, providing just enough to give the novel authenticity and establish it in time and space.

Overall it's not a bad novel. I'd even say it's a fairly good novel. The author seems intelligent and knowledgeable about human nature. He must be a very interesting person. I'd like to meet him sometime.

Tracking The Wolf Pack has been republished under my real name in paperback and as ebooks. I have rewritten the novel to get rid of all my criticisms mentioned above.

36

MY SECOND WAR SERIES

AFTER I FINISHED WRITING MY LAST NOVEL IN *THE Sergeant* series circa 1981, I needed another income stream ASAP. So I met with my new literary agent Barbara Lowenstein in her office on 57th Street between Broadway and 8th Avenue in Manhattan.

Barbara was approximately five feet tall, cute, energetic, thirty-something. I'd met her several years earlier when I was a press agent at the PR agency Solters & Sabinson, and she was one of Lee Solters's secretaries. Since then, she'd been a book editor and now reincarnated as a successful literary agent.

Paperback packager Jim Bryans, who'd recommended Barbara to me, referred to her as "the tiny terror".

After initial pleasantries, Barbara got right to the point. She asked what I intended to write next. I said another World War II series, this time about the Pacific war instead of the European War. Barbara was very professional, no nonsense, easy to talk with. She asked me to write the concept as a presentation which she'd try to sell.

I walked home to my nearby rundown studio pad on West 55th Street in the funky neighborhood known as Hell's Kitchen, lay on my sofa, gazed at paint peeling from the ceiling, and planned my new World War II series that I hoped would save me from the Municipal Men's Shelter, or a cardboard box beneath a bridge in Central Park.

I didn't want to simply transplant *The Sergeant* concept to the South Pacific island war. I wanted something as different as possible within the range of war novels. After much thought I decided that the new series would be about a whole platoon instead of one sergeant. But every platoon needs a sergeant so who would my new sergeant be?

Perhaps it was a failure of my imagination, but I could only come up with another rough and ready, no-nonsense, tactically-clever and somewhat brutal sergeant like Mazursky who made his grand debut in my first World War Two novel *Doom Platoon*, a standalone entry by pseudonym Richard Gallagher.

Mazursky did not vanish after *Doom Platoon*. Instead, he became the model for Sergeant Mahoney in my first World War Two series *The Sergeant* by Gordon Davis, originally published by Zebra beginning in 1980, then taken up by Bantam.

As mentioned previously, both Mazursky and Mahoney were inspired more or less by one of my best friends, Mike Nichols, a World War Two veteran and tough guy who grew up in Hell's Kitchen during the bad old days. Mike was not in the least afraid of violence, ready to rumble at any time, not opposed to threatening people in public places, quite scary when on a roll. He also happened to be a semi-criminal who had served eight years in a federal prison for attempting to smuggle a large quantity of marijuana from Mexico into Texas.

Mike's temper tantrums could be volcanic, but as I got to know him over the course of 30 years, came to realize that his horrific outbursts were mostly theater intended to achieve whatever results he wanted at the moment.

Why did I like him so? He was a genuinely interesting human being, a spellbinding conversationalist, party animal and raconteur par excellence. He died in 1993. My quality of life would be much improved if he still were alive. A framed photo of him stares at me as I write these words.

My next literary decision was: what would I call this new sergeant character? Because names matter and the name somehow must fit the character. Then I remembered a classmate of mine at Michigan State University. He was a big brawny moody guy from one of those steel towns near Pittsburgh, and his father worked in a steel mill. This classmate's name was Andrew P. Butsko which I always considered a great name and decided to use his last name for my new sergeant fighting in the Pacific war.

After formulating Sergeant Butsko's character, I needed to invent other characters in the platoon. I wanted them to be unique, not just ordinary guys. Finally I came up with:

A wild-ass cowboy from Texas who managed to display leadership qualities from time to time, who loved country music, usually was a cool head in battle, decent and honest most of the time, girl crazy like all young men, and would be a corporal under Butsko.

A Mafia hoodlum from Little Italy in Manhattan who

was violence prone, not patriotic in the least, displayed no leadership qualities whatever, hated the war and wished he'd never been drafted. His method of anger management was to punch someone, but Butsko often beats the shit out of him to keep him in line.

An Apache Indian from Arizona who was comfortable and resourceful in the outdoors, skilled at tracking and fighting.

A movie stuntman from Hollywood who could be relied upon for amazing physical feats.

An itinerant preacher from Georgia who tended to go berserk on the battlefield and considered himself the killer angel of God.

There were others but the above were the platoon's core. They got wounded from time to time but never were killed, as I recall. (It's been many years since I read every novel in the series.)

My next decision concerned exactly at what point in the Pacific war to begin the series. I finally chose the landings on Guadalcanal when American Marines and soldiers first began to take the fight to the Japanese Imperial Army instead of retreating.

My final decision concerned what to call the series. After much weighing of various possibilities I decided on *The Rat Bastards*. I thought this title might be too outrageous, but it sounded right according to my conception of the series, and certainly would be eye-catching on book racks in stores. My pseudonym would be John Mackie. I can't remember where this name came from. I think it just arose from the depths of my unconscious mind.

I wrote an overview and outlines for six novels and submitted them to Barbara, not knowing if anyone would bite. Then I returned home and worked on one of the standalone novels that I hoped would be my insurance policy if no one wanted to publish *The Rat Bastards*.

A short while later Barbara called to say Jove wanted to buy publishing rights, which skyrocketed my morale to the moon. She asked me to telephone my new editor, Damaris Rowland, or perhaps Damaris called me, I can't be sure after all these years.

I was not happy to learn that a woman would be editor of the series. What could a woman know about men's action/adventure novels? Finally I spoke with Damaris on the phone. She seemed friendly, gracious, complimentary and reasonable, definitely not a pain in the ass. She invited me to lunch at a restaurant in the East 30s.

I arrived at the appointed time and finally met Damaris face-to-face. She was in her thirties, taller than the average woman, slim, confident, elegant, sort of a Katherine Hepburn type. She turned out to be no ordinary New York woman. Her father had been an officer on General George Patton's staff during World War II, and her mother a young French woman caught up in the war. They met and fell in love during that hectic uncertain time.

Damaris grew up on Army posts all over the world, which meant she understood military life and the world of tough guys living under military discipline. Her exposure to many cultures made her a sophisticated, open-minded human being. She also had graduated from a prestigious college, don't remember the name. Against my deeply ingrained masculine prejudices, I decided she was eminently qualified to edit a male-oriented action/adventure series set during World War Two.

In the course of that first lunch, we told each other about ourselves and discovered that we both were mild-mannered, free-floating religious fanatics, admirers of Carl Jung and drawn to mystical aspects of religion, especially Hinduism, Buddhism and Zen.

It also turned out that we had similar tastes in literature. Damaris was as passionate about novels as I. She believed they ennobled the human race as did I. Another interesting wrinkle was that her sister was married to the mayor of Peekskill, New York, George Pataki, who later became Governor of New York state, and then a presidential contender!

After lunch with Damaris I went home and began about a month of intensive research, so I'd know what I was writing about. I learned that Japanese soldiers were even more fanatical than German soldiers. They believed their Emperor was an actual god and they were fighting a holy war. Death in battle was glorious by their standards, surrender dishonorable. How could ordinary American guys hope to defeat them?

Research always enthralled me but there came a point where I needed to stop reading and start writing the first novel in *The Rat Bastards* series, which I called *Hit The Beach!*

It became a massive bloody melodrama of going ashore under heavy fire, ferocious jungle fighting, snakes, swamps, crocodiles, malaria and leeches, told from viewpoints of both American and Japanese soldiers and officers, including guest appearances by historical figures such as Major General Alexander Vandegrift and Lieutenant General Harakuchi Hyakatuke.

Finally, I delivered the completed manuscript personally to Damaris. A short while later she said she loved it and thought it funny. She used the word "gut-bucket" to describe the genre in which she thought it belonged, and she was right because it was extraordinarily violent with lots of bloodshed and shattered bodies because I tried to be realistic about war and not pretty it up.

Damaris and I had many lunches together. We became good friends. She got married somewhere along the line, so I also became friendly with her husband, Joe. I even attended parties at their apartment in the East 20s.

I know what you're thinking – that Damaris and I had some kind of love affair. But we never were more than friends and literary collaborators. Usually we were involved with other people during those years. Besides, it's not a good idea to sleep with your editor or literary agent because when the relationship goes south, as relationships often do, at least in my life, editors and literary agents have the power and motivation to torpedo your literary career, and not a damned thing you can do about it.

Damaris told me that she read individual copies of *The Rat Bastards* right after they'd been published, often while riding the subway home. Sometimes she came upon scenes that made her laugh out loud, causing other subway riders to look at her curiously, as if she were nuts.

The Rat Bastards ran to 16 novels. They were thrilling to write and brought new levels of creativity out of me. I loved the covers and copy which announced:

YOU CAN'T KILL 'EM – AND YOU CAN'T TAKE 'EM ALIVE!

The Rat Bastards series still has many fans, which gladdens my heart. But the number one fan of the Rats will always be me.

Damaris and I remained friends after *The Rat Bastards*. We both finally left NYC but have stayed in touch via email. Wherever she is, whatever she's doing, she always will be top of the line.

The Rat Bastards series has been republished as ebooks under my real name Len Levinson.

37

MY FIRST WESTERN

IN 1985, AFTER I COMPLETED THE 16TH NOVEL IN MY *THE Rat Bastards* World War Two series by pseudonym John Mackie, published by Jove, the contract was not renewed presumably due to dismal sales. That rejection deeply demoralized me but more important than my feelings and vanity, the rejection severely impacted my finances because I had no source of income other than writing novels.

Obviously I needed a sit-down with my literary agent Barbara Lowenstein ASAP. Her office at that time was on West 57th Street near Broadway. I lived a short distance away on West 55th Street between 8th & 9th Avenues in the neighborhood known as Hell's Kitchen.

Barbara was and remains a no-nonsense business executive. She always was perfectly dressed and groomed, correct posture; I never saw her slouching in a chair. After initial hellos and how are yous, she asked the most important no-nonsense question: "What do you want to do next?"

I told her that I didn't know but would rather not write more war novels.

She thought for a few moments, then said, "Would you be interested in writing Westerns?"

A desperate writer cannot be choosy so you know very well my response: "Yes."

She replied with something like, "I'll see what I can do."

I walked home and resumed work on one of the standalone novels that I hoped would propel me to the very forefront of American literature, possibly becoming a best-seller, even winning the National Book Award. All eventually were published but none ever propelled me anywhere.

A short while after our meeting, Barbara called to say she had negotiated a contract for me to write two Western novels in the *Long Rider* series by Clay Dawson, to be published by Charter, a subsidiary of Berkley.

Thus did I become a Western writer although I lived in Manhattan, never rode a horse, never fired a six-gun or owned a cowboy hat.

But I was not totally ignorant about the Old West because I loved Western movies, TV shows and novels since my earliest years.

I grew up in New Bedford, Massachusetts. As a pre-teen I and my friends usually went to the movies at least once per week. We often watched "B" Westerns starring Hopalong Cassidy, Johnny Mack Brown, Sunset Carson, Lash Larue, and Wild Bill Elliott among others.

As I grew older, I saw many "A" Westerns starring John Wayne, Randolph Scott, Henry Fonda, Jimmy Stewart, Gregory Peck, Alan Ladd, etc., including Westerns directed by the great John Ford.

Also during my early impressionable years, I read

Zane Gray, Frank Gruber, Max Brand, Ernest Haycox, and several other writers, including a series that I especially liked as a teenager, *The Bar 20 Boys* by Clarence Mulford, which introduced the character of Hopalong Cassidy. One of my all-time favorite songs was and remains *Ghost Riders In The Sky*. I still remember most of the words and can sing it upon request but never receive requests, which probably is a good thing.

I was given a copy of the concept for the *Long Rider* series but no plot outlines. I'd need to invent my own plots. That was fine with me. I'd rather write my own plots than try to follow someone else's.

After studying and thinking about the concept, I sat down to write. The main character's name was Gabe Conrad. In my imagination he was entering a hotel room at night. Naturally he needed to turn on the light. *Wait a minute!* Exactly what kind of light did he turn on? Did he light a candle with a match? Were there matches in those days? Did he light a kerosene lamp? Whale oil lamp? Certainly no electricity was available in a small frontier town circa 1870. Was there wallpaper in the room? A wash basin and pitcher full of water? What kind of gun did he carry? How did it work?

I realized that I knew very few specifics about the Old West, therefore could not write about it with any degree of authenticity. What to do? The obvious solution was one of my favorite activities: research.

Every morning thereafter for about a month I walked to the public library on 5th Avenue and 42nd Street, climbed marble stairs to massive room 315, which was the main reading room, requested and read historical works about the Old West, some quite rare. I lunched in the neighborhood, returned to the library until dinner time, then walked home.

While sitting in room 315 with college students, other types of researchers, guys reading racing newspapers, mentally disturbed stinky homeless individuals mumbling to themselves, and other scholars, I soon realized that many men in the Old West were Civil War veterans, so I needed to study the Civil War in greater depth if I wanted to understand them. But in order to understand the Civil War, I needed to study the Mexican War. And in order to understand the Mexican War I needed to study the War of 1812.

I finally accepted that in order to fully understand the Old West, I needed to go back to the American Revolution and comprehend how America came to be and what were its underlying assumptions. I realized that Westerns actually were historical novels. I couldn't just wing it, because people who read westerns understood the territory and would spot errors instantly.

Thus began my love affair with American history which continues to this day. Some of those books that I read were quite absorbing. I think my favorite was *The Trail Drivers Of Texas* by J. Marvin Hunter who interviewed many old cowboys who had worked the cattle drives from Texas to the Kansas railheads, sleeping in the wide open, fighting rustlers, other types of outlaws, hostile Indians, tornados and other obstacles all the way, keeping their herds bunched and pointed north, butchering steers regularly for their diet staple, broiled or stewed meat.

I also especially liked *Roughing It* by Mark Twain, his memoir of living in a Nevada mining town after the Civil War, and consisting mostly of amusing and sometimes even hilarious anecdotes about all the gold-crazed lunatics, swindlers and insane situations that he encountered there. I considered *Roughing It* much better than

Huckleberry Finn and *Tom Sawyer*. It inspired me to set my first *Long Rider* novel in a gold mining town.

I also read many other classics of Western history, and many Western novels. My favorite Western author became Louis L'Amour whose characters had toughness, roughness and a sense of honor that I hoped to emulate.

Tribal people then known as Indians were part of the Old West, so I needed to study them also. I wanted in-depth knowledge but didn't have time to research all Western tribes thoroughly so decided to focus on just one, the most ferocious of them all, the mighty Apaches, and dig as deep as I could.

In pursuit of this goal, I read many books about Apache culture. The best was *An Apache Lifeway* by Morris Opler, an anthropologist from the University of Chicago who lived among the Apaches in the 1920s and 1930s and interviewed many old warriors, or children of old warriors who had fought under Mangas Coloradas, Victorio, Cochise and Geronimo. Opler detailed much authoritative info about Apaches from birth to death and was indispensable to my research.

Geronimo's autobiography also was immensely useful. He was a medicine man in addition to warrior chieftain and provided an insider view of the very strange (to me) Apache religion.

Finally, it was time to stop reading and start writing. I decided against my original opening scene of Gabe entering a hotel room at night. Instead, he was riding into a gold mining town on a hot summer day. Of course there would be shootouts, punchouts, horses galloping here and there, and all other accouterments of Western novels, but mainly I needed to tell an interesting story because that was the goal of everything I ever wrote.

Opportunities for drama in Western novels appeared

LEN LEVINSON

endless. I really enjoyed writing them. But I should make
clear that writing novels wasn't simply writing novels, at
least for me. It was like living in novels and being whatever character I was writing at the moment, like having
innumerable incarnations and becoming more than just
plain Lenny Levinson. I felt like a god creating entire
worlds and loved the feeling.

I went on to write a total of 26 Westerns. They were
happy days for me. I was riding the range in my imagination, while sitting in my funky Manhattan apartment
in the Hell's Kitchen neighborhood.

During my Western writing career, I took several
research trips to Western states, visited an Apache reservation in Arizona, hiked to the ruins of Fort Apache,
walked the streets of Tombstone, wandered around the
Sonoran Desert with sandwiches and two canteens full
of water in my backpack, bought cowboy shirts and even
a cowboy hat.

I really got into writing Western novels. They were a
great ride. I'm very glad that necessity forced me to write
them. I never would have written any Westerns on my
own. The notion never would have occurred to me.
Thank goodness for necessity.

One could say accurately that all my 86 published
novels were inspired by necessity combined with love of
writing and living in stories. In those days I felt confident that I could write virtually anything. And I did.

38

MY FIRST WESTERN SERIES

WHILE WRITING TWO WESTERN NOVELS IN THE *LONG Rider* series for Berkley circa 1986, I was enjoying myself so much, I wanted to create and write my very own Western series.

What would it be?

The Old West offered unlimited dramatic possibilities. First, I needed to come up with a character, then plots would follow. Who exactly was he? What would be the name of his game?

According to my research, the Old West was populated with many people seeking new opportunities on the great American frontier. Some were farmers wanting inexpensive land; or entrepreneurs planning to start businesses; or criminals running from police back east; or innumerable adventurous types searching for excitement which was plentiful in the new land, perhaps too plentiful; and finally a great number of Civil War veterans hoping to forget the bloody mess they recently had survived.

After weighing various choices, I finally decided that

my main character would be some kind of Civil War veteran, and the series would begin shortly after the end of that titanic struggle.

What side had he fought on? Gradually I was drawn to the notion of a Confederate cavalry officer who'd lost everything in the war and hoped for a new life on the frontier.

Why a Confederate instead of a Union officer? Perhaps because often I too felt like I was on the losing side of a war, in my case my war to achieve financial stability as a freelance novelist.

I perceived my ex-Confederate officer as a tragically romantic figure, something of an intellectual, emotionally sensitive beneath his rugged exterior, but whenever there was violence in his vicinity, as so often happened on the frontier, the old war craziness came over him and he became quite dangerous.

So who would he be already? I had to get specific and make a final decision.

I really can't explain point by point how the creative process works inside my skull, but visions or hallucinations play a part. I was starting to visualize a big guy in his late twenties, around six-foot-four, broad shoulders, flat stomach, wearing a beat-up old Confederate cavalry officer's wide brimmed hat, walking into a frontier saloon in the first paragraph of the first page of the first novel.

What was his backstory? Because he needed a backstory in order for me to see him as a fully realized flesh and blood human being. Details of his backstory might not appear chronologically in novels but were necessary for my own understanding of him.

Gradually the pieces fell into place. I imagined that his father had owned a vast plantation in South Carolina with many slaves. My protagonist never was involved with day-to-day management, never bought or sold slaves, never worked as an overseer, never raped slave women.

Instead, he had been just another frivolous young Southern aristocrat who spent most of his time riding and racing horses, hunting on horseback, fishing, gambling, going to balls at opulent mansions, playing sports, attending a succession of private schools, and occasionally drinking more than was good for him.

Like many other Southerners including Robert E. Lee, he was troubled by the "peculiar institution" of slavery but couldn't imagine how he personally could change anything, so preferred to look the other way toward his pleasures, devotion to his family, his love life, and ambition to attend West Point.

Not everyone is a militant. Not everyone is an activist. Many dislike and avoid politics. Some even hate politics. My protagonist was one of these.

What was his name? Because names of protagonists are important. They've got to have a certain ring. I thought of many possibilities but had to choose one.

Somehow an old song by the Beach Boys was echoing through the tunnels of my mind at that time. It contained the lyrics:

> *Sheriff John Stone*
> *Why don't you leave me alone?*

That's it, I thought. I'll call him John Stone.

I didn't want him wandering the frontier aimlessly like a bum. I wanted his life to have purpose and meaning. What more than anything else gives men purpose and meaning?

Women.

I knew this for a fact personally because at that time I'd recently been involved with a certain young lady named Marie. After four years together we broke up for the same reason most couples break up. Our incompatibilities gradually outweighed our compatibilities. But we really loved each other underneath it all. As I look back, I believe that no one ever loved me like Marie, and I guess she was the great love of my life.

She left NYC and went West after we broke up. I missed her very much while I was planning my new Western series. She was in my heart and mind so often she became part of the series.

I reinvented her as a young lady also named Marie who grew up on a plantation near the Stone plantation. She and John Stone had known each other nearly all their lives and loved each other most of that time. It was taken for granted by them and their families that they would marry after John graduated from West Point. Their future appeared lovely except for one big problem: the impending crisis that became the Civil War.

John was in his last year at West Point when South Carolinians fired on Fort Sumter. Like many West Pointers he had conflicting loyalties. His close friend and classmate George Armstrong Custer from Michigan stayed with the Union Army, but John remained loyal to South Carolina. He simply could not go to war against his native land and felt morally compelled to defend South Carolina from the coming Northern invasion, despite misgivings about slavery.

He returned home and enlisted in the Hampton Legion, a cavalry unit formed by Wade Hampton also from South Carolina, one of the wealthiest plantation owners in the South whom John Stone and his family knew personally. The Hampton Legion later became the Hampton Brigade.

Lieutenant John Stone became Captain John Stone during what Southerners called "The War of Northern Aggression". He fought in the bloodiest battles of that great conflict, numerous friends had been killed, he had been painfully wounded on several occasions, carried scars all over his body, and it was all for naught. The surrender totally demoralized him, but the worst was yet to come.

He returned home after mustering out and discovered that his parents had died recently, the plantation mansion burned to the ground, fields devastated. To make matters worse, if possibly there could be something worse: the family plantation has been deeply in debt and reclaimed by the bank. He had no money to speak of and no idea of what to do with himself.

What about Marie? She had disappeared. John was told she went west with a Union officer. John couldn't believe Marie went anywhere with a Union officer. With nothing better to do, he went West to search for her. All he had was his Army horse, his Army revolver, his old Confederate cavalry officer's hat, his love for Marie, and an old Daguerreotype of her which he will show people along the way, asking if they've seen her.

John Stone arrives in a Kansas town on the first page of the first novel in the series. Parts of his backstory will be told from time to time in memories, flashbacks and exposition inserted whenever necessary as he journeys deeper into the wild frontier. Wherever he goes, he inquires about Marie and shows the Daguerreotype of her.

Sometimes unprincipled people purposely send him on wild goose chases for the hell of it. Others honestly believe they've seen Marie but are mistaken. John meets a rancher's wife who looks just like her but becomes disappointed again.

Working at odd jobs to support himself, he becomes sheriff of a small town for a while, is employed as a cowboy for a spell, and rides the drag on a cattle drive from Texas to Kansas. Wherever he is, whatever he does, he's always searching for the great love of his life.

Sometimes he gets discouraged but never gives up. Naturally the series includes lots of gunfights, fistfights, knife fights and other action because the Wild West was not a peaceful place. John Stone even runs into his old friend George Armstrong Custer at an Army fort way out there on the frontier.

I decided to call my new Western series *Searcher* because it seemed the most accurate title. I was aware of the movie *The Searchers* starring John Wayne, which I had seen and enjoyed, but my series was so different, I didn't think there'd be confusion between the two.

My literary agent Barbara Lowenstein sold my *Searcher* concept to Charter Diamond. My editor became Tom Colgan who seemed to really like the series. Eventually it became twelve novels by Josh Edwards. I became very emotionally involved with *Searcher* and was exceedingly disappointed when the final contract wasn't renewed. I wanted to keep going for many more novels, but the party suddenly was over.

I assumed that Charter Diamond's decision was based on low sales but recently learned it probably was because they considered *Searcher* an Adult Western.

Walmart and other family-oriented retail outlets decided to stop selling Adult Westerns, so some publishers stopped publishing them. That included

Searcher although it contained no triple XXX-rated hardcore pornography.

Admittedly *Searcher* characters sometimes became passionate about each other and occasionally went to bed together because *Searcher* was about real human beings, not a Western fairy tale. I didn't describe body parts or fornication details, but Charter Diamond execs evidently classified *Searcher* as adult Westerns so scratched me off their lists.

The original twelve novels have been republished as ebooks under my real name, Len Levinson.

39

MY ALL-TIME FAVORITE
WESTERN NOVEL

STAMPEDE WAS MY ALL-TIME FAVORITE WESTERN NOVEL that I ever wrote. It was #7 in my *Searcher* series published in 1992 by Charter Diamond under my pseudonym Josh Edwards.

Set shortly after the Civil War, *Stampede* tells of a cattle drive from Texas to a railhead in Kansas and stars my hero/anti-hero protagonist John Stone, a former Confederate cavalry officer searching for his lost love Marie in the Wild West and working at odd jobs to support himself.

Stampede was inspired by one of the best books I ever read about the Wild West, *The Trail Drivers Of Texas* by J. Marvin Hunter, mentioned previously and consisting of interviews with cowboys who'd actually worked on cattle drives and coped with rustlers, other types of outlaws, hostile Indians, tornadoes, stampedes and numerous additional difficulties while keeping their herds together and moving steadily north toward railheads in Kansas.

Stampede also was influenced by the old TV series

Rawhide about cattle drives and starring young Clint Eastwood. *Stampede* additionally was fertilized by one of the greatest Western movies ever made, *Red River*, another cattle drive extravaganza starring the unbeatable combination of John Wayne and Montgomery Clift, directed by Howard Hawks.

My *Stampede* is very different from *Rawhide* and *Red River* because it erupted from my own personal feverish imagination which was extra-feverish when I was writing *Stampede*.

I always get deeply involved with my novels but somehow became more deeply involved than usual with this one. Sometimes I felt like I was plugged into the wall along with my computer, causing high voltage sparking through my veins and around my cranium.

I passionately loved writing this novel. It has everything a cattle drive novel should have, every type of tribulation, violence and catastrophe but also includes comedy, love and even, believe it or not, a peyote trip in which John Stone and the other cowboys get stoned out of their skulls at a crucial point in the cattle drive.

Love? The herd is owned by a young woman named Cassandra and she too is on the cattle drive. She's an orphan and widow who married Mister Wrong who ruined her financially, and her only hope for economic recovery is to get the cattle to market in Kansas. She resembles John Stone's lost love Marie so a certain attraction builds between them, but I won't divulge what happens because I shouldn't spoil the story for anyone who might want to read it.

Cassandra always has led a sheltered life and is not equipped to deal with ex-criminals, lunatics and tough guys who are working the cattle drive, especially the ramrod Truscott who calls her Clarabelle and actually laughs at her whenever she orders him to do something. The grizzled cowboys all treat her like an idiot or dizzy child and do as they damn well please but Cassandra has true grit, adapts to the situation, and eventually gains control of them. It ain't easy and I won't tell you how because again, I shouldn't spoil the story for anyone who might want to read it.

The cook is a former slave who in those days was called a Negro. By an odd quirk of fate, he had been a field slave on John Stone's father's plantation and hates John Stone intensely although Stone barely remembers him and had nothing to do with management of the plantation; he usually was away at private boarding schools and finally West Point. John Stone and the former slave are on a deadly collision course and eventually will fight it out, white man and black man trying to kill each other or be killed.

The first paragraphs on the first page are:

The cowboys from the Triangle Spur sat around the campfire, eating steak and beans. It was night, a chill was on the prairie, and the indigo sky was splattered with stars. The men were exhausted, clothes torn, fingernails caked with dirt. On the trail nearly a week, it was a constant struggle to keep the longhorns shaped, bunched and pointed toward Abilene.

Near the flames, John Stone leaned against his saddle, his old Confederate cavalry hat on the back of his head. His clothes were covered with dust which permeated his dark blond hair and beard. This was his first cattle drive, and he rode the drag.

The other cowboys were as tattered and beat as he. They were the usual assortment of misfits, vagabonds, adventurers and desperadoes, firelight flickering on their bearded faces because nobody had the time, energy, or inclination to shave. Some had driven long-horns to Abilene before, while others like Stone were making their first trip. They knew that hardship lay ahead, and other cowboys had died violently on the trail, ending up in lonely graves on the trackless wastes, but so far the drive had been without incident.

It won't be without incident much longer because this is after all a Len Levinson Western.

Later in my Western literary career, a guy named Acklin Hoofman from Michigan contacted me and we spoke on the phone a few times. He collected Westerns, had amassed a huge collection, and asked if I'd autograph some of mine that he owned. I said yes, he mailed them to me, I signed and mailed them back.

During one of our conversations, we spoke about *Stampede*. Acklin Hoofman said, "A book like that doesn't come along every day."

The *Searcher* series has been republished as ebooks under my real name, Len Levinson.

40

THE GO-GO DANCER AND THE PARROT

BACK IN THE 1980S WHEN I LIVED IN NEW YORK CITY and was writing pulp fiction novels for a living, I had a buddy whom I'll call Roxy because I don't want to embarrass her by using her real name.

She was a go-go dancer who worked in NYC night clubs and told me she often earned $500.00 per night! Many fans followed her from club to club, making her a star on the Big Apple go-go circuit. Roxy was around five feet two inches tall and somewhat resembled young Bette Davis, although I'm sure she'd disagree.

A talented gymnast as a child, Roxy majored in Theater Arts and Dance at a major American university, graduated with a Bachelor's degree, relocated on a shoe-string to NYC, found work as a go-go dancer, and got accepted at the Actor's Studio, the same school that taught the acting ropes to Marlon Brando, Paul Newman, Marilyn Monroe, Jack Nicholson, Al Pacino, Robert De Niro, etc.

Roxy appeared in many Off-Off Broadway plays that I attended. Whenever on stage, she was center of gravity even when not speaking. Her ability to express character through gestures, facial expressions and pure psychological intensity were amazing. Her lines were delivered believably as if from a real person, not a trained stage actress with artificial speech patterns and studied mannerisms. I thought she was a wonderful actress but competition in the theater world is ferocious, and unfortunately Roxy didn't interview well.

Essentially Roxy was shy and modest in everyday life. In interviews she didn't project the same confidence and authority that made her outstanding on stage. She also felt uncomfortable trying to sell herself to busy casting directors.

We met at a mutual friend's apartment in the Hell's Kitchen neighborhood where we all lived. Roxy and I became good friends. Often we hung out together, smoked certain dried leaves and buds then illegal, and discussed all manner of subjects. She was especially interested in astrology and other occult practices which she called "hoodoo-voodoo".

Twice I went to nightclubs and watched her perform. Other go-go dancers did the basic bump and grind, but Roxy was a university-trained dancer. She choreographed elaborate dance routines for herself, sometimes incorporating gymnastics, and really put on artistic performances that outshone the bumpers and grinders and drew her a devoted following, like the Judy Garland of go-go dancers.

After watching one of Roxy's performances, I wrote a poem:

GO-GO GIRL

Her feet go jumping

and her feathers kick around
boobies bouncing
up and down
And her painted face
is the painted face
of a pretty harlequin clown
And sometimes
oh boy
She can really get down
And the guys sit around
in that corner of hell
leering
dreaming
burning for the girl
with the feathered feet
hipping and bopping
the night away
And she's not even there
No, she's not even there
uh uh, not her
her mind's on the edge
of a far-off star
and she's got this smile
and she's got those eyes
that have seen the bottom
and have seen the highs
And you can glimpse her courage
You can sense her pride
You can feel her magic
all the while
as you watch her
go-go going
go-go going
And sometimes

oh boy
She can really get down

Occasionally Roxy and I wandered Manhattan together. One day on the upper East Side near 86th Street and Lexington Avenue we came upon a pet shop. Roxy loved animals so we entered. She inclined toward dogs while I wandered around aimlessly peering at critters in cages or tanks. It looked like they were in the equivalent of supermax prison. I didn't think they were very happy.

Then I came upon a green parrot in a cage. He was looking intently at me. I drew closer and felt that he was evaluating me. Who knows what sensibilities parrots have? Perhaps he was trying to communicate on the subliminal wavelength, or only monitoring movement in his vicinity?

He seemed proud, stalwart, intelligent, and there he was locked in a cage. I wondered how he got there. Probably trapped in some South American jungle. So this elegant bird accustomed to flying free in emerald forests, eating fruit and seeds, now was incarcerated in a tiny cage. What a horrible tragedy to befall a beautiful intelligent creature.

You know what happened next, ladies and gentlemen. You know that a brand-new literary idea popped into my so-called brain. I felt inspired to write a novel about a parrot in a pet shop who is bought by a go-go dancer, then sold and bought numerous times by various people whom he observes closely, learning their stories. I would call the novel *The Parrot*, the narrative told from his point of view.

I felt electrified by this story concept and after returning home, began working on it. In back of my mind was *E.T. The Extraterrestrial*, the movie novelization written by my old buddy, William Kotzwinkle whom I've already mentioned.

I considered Bill's *E.T.* book much better than *E.T.* the movie because Bill's book was more adult oriented, not a cutesy-poo kiddie show like the movie. Bill's E.T. character was a botanist from another planet, a scientist left behind by mistake, forcing him to figure out logically his new bewildering and dangerous world. Bill's singular imagination made the novel a sensation which helps explain why it was number one international best seller of the 1980s.

I conceived my parrot as a character essentially like E.T., a stranger in a strange land trying to figure it out. I described parrots as masters of communication who learned other languages easily and actually could talk, not just fake "Polly wanna cracker" routines. Of course parrots dare not talk openly with humans because they figured humans couldn't accept an actual conversational parrot. The humans might go berserk and even kill the parrot. As I presented parrots, they also knew how to read minds and communicate silently on the subliminal wavelength.

I did a lot of research on birds in general and parrots in particular, discovering that African Gray Parrots were considered smartest parrot species of all. So I made my parrot an African Gray who even learned to read newspapers placed in the bottom of his cage to catch his droppings, enabling him to become more acquainted with his new world.

My friend Roxy became inspiration for the go-go dancer who buys the parrot, but I spun my fictional go-go dancer as much crazier and erratic than Roxy for the sake of drama, conflict and all other requirements of a novel.

My go-go character used drugs and booze excessively, which Roxy didn't. My character had many meltdowns, unlike Roxy who was a tough little chick in control of her life most of the time, although she probably didn't think so.

Roxy owned a sewing machine and designed and made her own costumes which were very theatrical and imaginative. So were her cosmetics. Once I was in her pad while she was applying mascara before going to work. She said, while looking in the mirror and highlighting her eyes, "When you're a woman – every day is Halloween." I never forgot that line and used it in the parrot novel and a few other novels.

My fictional go-go dancer's wild and sometimes lurid shenanigans were observed carefully by my fictional astute parrot. Finally the dancer sold him, don't remember why. Many different kinds of people then buy and sell him. Some are nice. Some not so nice. He even gets into a war with a very nasty cat who is jealous of him.

Finally the parrot gets desperate and talks to his last owner who is a scientist and not too crazy. After recovering from the jolt of a parrot communicating verbally with him, the scientist takes the bird back to Africa and turns him loose. The end.

I spent many months working on this novel, had no income while writing it, used my savings to pay bills, and savings weren't much to begin with. In other words, I was writing on spec, gambling with my life as usual, living frugally by necessity, because I loved the story concept.

Finally I finished the parrot novel, rewrote and edited it several times, but ultimately was not satisfied. Somehow it didn't jell, probably because the story simply wasn't very believable, and worst of all, wasn't very interesting. Somehow, I was unable to execute my great parrot idea. Perhaps that level of fantasy was beyond my ability. Perhaps I was at my best when writing about people shooting, stabbing, punching, kicking and blasting each other to smithereens with high-grade explosives. So my great American parrot novel became another financial and career setback.

Not every writer sells every novel. Even famous successful writers occasionally write flops. This was one of mine. What did I do next? Continue writing pulp fiction – what else?

Roxy and I still are good friends although we no longer live in NYC and have ended up around twelve hundred miles apart. But she always will be my little buddy and I always will love her as one of my best friends ever. As could be expected, she became quite a hit in regional theater. She also married an excellent guy. They live with a gang of dogs. Roxy always loved dogs.

A few years ago, I came across the manuscript of *The Parrot* and reread it in the hope that I'd see clearly how to fix it after all these years, but it still didn't work as a story or anything else. I couldn't figure out how to fix it.

Some things just can't be fixed, but *The Parrot* was a worthwhile effort because it taught me a few lessons about writing and myself. Everything that happens to a writer is grist for the mill. Nothing ever is wasted in the long run. For example, *The Parrot* inspired this chapter.

41

MY GREAT AMERICAN CRACK-UP

...OR LENNY GETS LOCKED IN A PSYCHO WARD

THIS IS NOT A HAPPY CHAPTER. PERHAPS YOU SHOULD proceed to the next chapter if you get easily depressed, or if you're on the edge of suicide.

There came a point in the 1980s when I was slammed with a series of four catastrophes that landed me in the Bronx Veterans Administration hospital psycho ward. These catastrophes were:

#1. Cancellation of my *Searcher* series demoralized me considerably. Then I wrote *The Parrot* and some other novels that I couldn't sell and was running out of money, which caused obsessive worry about relocating to the Municipal Men's Shelter or a cardboard box beneath a bridge in Central Park.

I couldn't help thinking that my so-called literary career had been a mistake, failure and bad joke. This notion shook me to the depths of my being, which evidently was not as deep as I'd thought, otherwise my books would have been published and I would have wider readership and more money.

#2. I still felt lost without Marie, my former girl-friend and great love of my life. Somehow, I couldn't get over her. She ended our four-year relationship primarily because she was around 22 years younger than I and wanted children, whereas I didn't want more children. She also probably wanted someone around her age, who had something that resembled a future, instead of a middle-aged depressed balding man having difficulty paying his basic bills. I still loved her very much and felt bereft without her but didn't blame her for leaving me. I wasn't the best boyfriend who ever lived, because I was and remain a temperamental artist.

#3. I was diagnosed with tumors of the parathyroid glands and underwent surgery at Mount Sinai Hospital. After surgery I was wheeled on a gurney to a dingy little room with grim view of an airshaft. In this room I contemplated death in all its ramifications. I always knew that I was going to die someday but death never seemed so close before. The prospect of death horribly concentrated my mind, frightened me and transformed my thinking forevermore.

#4. My close friend Gloria committed suicide. I was unable to cope with this tragic event. We never had been lovers but spent much time together, knew each other's secrets and were very attuned to each other psychologically and intellectually. She once said that we were "like sister and brother". Her suicide shattered my world and sent me into a downward spiral from which, combined with factors mentioned above, I could not pull out of.

Gloria had been depressed on and off since child-hood although she came from an affluent background, but money evidently does not protect people from depression. During the twenty-odd years that I knew her, she bounced from one terrible love affair to another. Finally, she became involved with a professor of mathematics who said he'd marry her, then a few months later changed his mind and Gloria discovered he was carrying on with another woman.

She couldn't handle it so swallowed a lot of pills. I was in Maine at the time, staying at the home of Bill and Elizabeth Kotzwinkle. Soon after returning home, I clicked on my telephone answering machine. Among the messages was Gloria's voice. I'll never forget her plea:

"Len – if you're there, please pick up the phone. I really need you now, Len."

I immediately called Gloria. She didn't answer. I called one of her girlfriends and asked if she knew where Gloria was.

Her friend paused, then said angrily, "Gloria is dead!"

She told me the awful story. I felt like I'd been run over by the A train. I couldn't accept Gloria's suicide and became enveloped in a cloud of negative downbound thought. Gloria had been a very intelligent person. If she didn't think life was worth living – perhaps life really wasn't worth living?

I felt overwhelmed by Gloria's and my own tragedy. I barely could function. My whole world seemed to be falling apart. It wasn't long before I began contemplating suicide as a reasonable career alternative. Why not simply off myself and end the pain?

One evening, while watching *Out Of Africa* on tv, I couldn't tolerate my wretchedness any longer. I opened the window and looked six floors down to pavement of the back alley behind my apartment building. Surely the drop would be sufficient to fracture my skull and kill me. I leaned out the window and closed my eyes. All I needed to do was push a little with my toes, and that would be the end of my unhappy screwed-up life.

At the last moment I became frightened by my thoughts. I imagined myself smashed to bits on the pavement below, blood exploding in all directions. It finally occurred to me that I needed help. I had no family in the NYC area except a half-brother whom I didn't see much because he recently had married and was busy with his job and new marriage. He and my friends all had their own problems, and I didn't want to add to their burdens. I definitely didn't want anyone to say, "You're bringin' me down, man," or, "You're dumpin' on me, man."

My only reasonable course of action was to walk to the Roosevelt Hospital emergency room conveniently located only three blocks away, the very emergency room where John Lennon died. I approached the front desk and told the nurse, "I'm thinking about committing suicide."

Next thing I knew, I was escorted by security staff to a nearby small, padded room with no windows. I had to empty my pockets and give them everything including my belt and shoelaces. Then the security staff locked me in.

I immediately became claustrophobic. Now I was locked up, as if I didn't have enough problems already. My freedom had been taken away! What had I done to myself? All my civil rights suddenly gone I had no idea what would happen to me. It appeared that I had gone from the pressure cooker into the flames.

After approximately one hour, security staff opened the door and led me to an office in which sat two women mental health professionals. One was probably in her 60s, wizened, gray hair, very serious, even stern. The other was in her 20s, quite pretty, apparently very concerned about me.

The old shrink asked questions in a cold, accusatory heavy-duty European accent. I felt that she didn't like me and even had contempt for me, which I considered justified in view of my many stupid decisions and failures over the years. In stark contrast, the young shrink seemed very warm and compassionate.

I figured that the old shrink was the young shrink's supervisor, and the old shrink was planning to have me locked in some psychiatric hospital, probably Bellevue, and throw away the key. I could not allow that to happen. I'd much prefer to be suicidal in my own apartment, thank you very much.

So I smiled and told them that I felt much better, my suicidal thoughts had gone away, and I'd like to go home now if they didn't mind. The young shrink seemed to agree but the old shrink was not convinced, so I laid it on even thicker, telling them that my emergency room experience had caused a major reconsideration of my values. Suicide no longer seemed a reasonable solution to my problems, which appeared not so serious in retrospect, and I would never, never, *never* commit suicide.

Finally, they turned me loose. I retrieved my belongings and walked home. But I had lied. My inclination to suicide had not vanished. In days to come, as my mental deterioration continued, I decided that I still needed help.

So I rode the subway to the Bronx VA hospital where I received my usual medical care from Dr. Mark Korsten in the gastrointestinal department. This time I made my way to the psychiatric department and told the person behind the desk that I wanted to talk with someone because I was contemplating suicide.

The person behind the desk invited me to take a seat. I expected security guards to arrive and lock me in another padded cell. Instead, a heavyset white male psychiatrist in his thirties showed up with a clip board. He had slicked down black hair, pencil mustache, wore pleated pants, brown and white saddle-style shoes, and looked like a ladies' man.

He led me to a large, empty meeting room. I told him what I was going through. He took notes, asked a few questions, rendered no verdicts, offered no advice, wrote on his clipboard, and after a while excused himself, presumably to confer with his superiors about exactly what padded cell to lock me in.

I sat and fidgeted awhile, then the shrink came back and led me to the office of the number one psychiatrist at the Bronx VA.

He probably was in his fifties, Jewish like me, average height and build, beard trimmed in the style favored by Mephistopheles in paintings and cartoons. Dr. Mephistopheles asked several questions about my predicament, and I responded as accurately as possible.

He listened intently, then explained that he and his staff were conducting experiments with depressed people. The experiments consisted of swallowing pills and/or receiving injections of various medications that hopefully would alleviate depression. The pills and/or injections would be combined with talk therapy and careful monitoring of results. He thought these treatments would help me recover my psychological equilibrium. Then came the kicker. Patients being studied would need to get locked in the psycho ward so all variables could be controlled.

I was so desperate I was willing to endure anything if

I could be normal again. So I agreed to get locked in the Bronx VA psycho ward!

I went home and packed a few articles. Next morning, I reported like a good cooperative psychiatric patient on time to the psycho ward. I remember stopping at the front desk and signing a lot of papers. Then an aide escorted me into the psycho ward. When he locked the door behind us, my first gut reaction was that I had just landed myself in doo-doo much deeper than usual.

I tried to ignore these gut feelings and hoped for the best. Perhaps the experiments would cure me. The aide showed me my bed and locker in a room with three other beds. He left, I unpacked, then wandered around the psycho ward in order to acquaint myself with my lovely new surroundings.

It looked like any other bleak hospital ward except the entrance door was locked. Corridors were lined with rooms like mine, there was a community room, and lots of psychiatric patients wandering about.

The first thing I noticed was that many patients seemed heavily medicated and glassy eyed like zombies. I probably would be just like them in a few days, but it might be better than suicidal ideations.

I looked into a room and saw a guy who evidently was Jewish because he wore a prayer shawl and was ostentatiously davening while mumbling what I presumed were prayers from a book held in both hands. "Davening" means rocking back and forth in rhythm to prayers because Jews are commanded to pray not just with words but with their bodies. Oddly, he wore a cowboy hat instead of a yarmulke. He looked completely out of place in the psycho ward, as if I were hallucinating.

Later in the day I spoke with him. I don't remember details of our conversation, but my impression was that he was acting crazy in order to receive increased disability payments from the VA, and really was not as crazy as he appeared.

I was not feeling very happy in the psycho ward. In fact, it was making me more depressed than I was already, because basically I was an introvert but couldn't escape other people in the psycho ward.

I gradually came to the conclusion that it probably wasn't a good idea for a depressed suicidal person like me to be among mentally disturbed people because the pathological atmosphere they projected intensified my feelings of being loco in the coco and weakened my already tenuous grip on reality. Their mental illness became my environment, reality and truth, which was not what I needed at that time. I needed calm, peaceful, normal surroundings.

Dinnertime with mental patients in harsh lighting was not exactly an exquisite dining experience like the Four Seasons or even the average Chinatown restaurant. I admitted to myself that I hated the psycho ward and had made a major mistake by checking myself into it voluntarily. Somehow, I had to get out.

It also occurred to me that I would spend the rest of my life in nightmarish psycho wards unless I woke up and started fighting for my life. My thoughts focused on escape from the psycho ward. Somehow suicide didn't seem so desirable anymore. I didn't want to die. I just wanted to be mentally healthy and strong again.

After dinner, I didn't know what to do with myself. No library was available on the psycho ward, only a tv room. I didn't like the tv show that other patients were watching. I was starting to feel panicky but couldn't go anywhere because I was locked into the psycho ward.

I played pool for a while with a young black guy who seemed heavily medicated, but somehow sank all his shots and beat me. Then I got into a conversation with a spidery little white guy who seemed very freaky with lots of facial twitches and odd psychomotor movement. Finally, he asked for twenty dollars. I turned him down. He became upset, narrowed his eyes, and ran his finger across his throat as if he planned to cut my throat.

The scar on my throat from parathyroid surgery still was fresh. He had spotted my vulnerability and zeroed in on it. I don't like to be scared. Paradoxically it makes me belligerent. After I threatened this creep with high levels of violence if he ever started up with me, I walked away.

I decided to go to bed and sleep it off, but my pillow was gone. Apparently, someone had stolen it, so I set off in search of it. Lo and behold I found it in the TV room. A lean young black woman was lying on a sofa with her head propped up on my pillow. Apparently, she had snatched it for her comfort.

One important lesson I learned in my hometown of New Bedford and in the Army was that I absolutely could not let people mess with me, otherwise it would never end. So I said something like, "That's my pillow. I want to go to bed. Please give me my pillow."

I made this statement straightforwardly, not shyly or meekly. I looked directly into her eyes so that she'd know I was serious. Without a word she raised her head, pulled away the pillow and held it the air.

I grabbed it, carried it to my bed, undressed, and crawled under the covers. The pillow smelled as if the young woman had not bathed for a significant period of time. After a while my roommates returned and prepared for bed. Soon it was lights out.

I lay in the darkness and thought, "I've got to get the hell out of here."

Next morning, I refused blood tests and medications which were part of the experiment I was supposed to be in. I found the psychiatrist on duty in the ward. She was black, slim, 40-something and seemed ill at ease in the psycho ward, as well she should have been because lunatics were wandering around and some might be dangerous.

I told her that I'd changed my mind and wanted to get out of the psycho ward ASAP. She replied that was impossible. I reminded her that I had signed myself in voluntarily, had done nothing wrong, therefore she couldn't keep me against my will. Again, she refused to release me. Evidently, she thought that my desire to depart the psycho ward was merely a symptom of my madness, and she shouldn't humor me.

I left her office, feeling trapped like a rat. What should I do? Then I remembered seeing a payphone in one of the halls. Fortunately, I had change in my pocket. I found the payphone, dropped the quarter, and dialed my gastroenterologist, Dr. Korsten. Thank God he came on the phone. I told him that I wanted to get out of the psycho ward but the staff wouldn't release me.

I remember his exact words (more or less). He said, "I never thought you should go into the psycho ward."

"Can you get me out?"

"I'll see what I can do."

I spoke with the psychiatrist on duty again, and again she refused to let me out because my request to leave obviously was a symptom of my madness.

I had another quarter so called Mike Nichols whom I've mentioned previously.

"How ya doin'," he asked.

"I'm in the Bronx VA psycho ward and can't get out."

"Why are you in a psycho ward?"

"I signed myself in."

He was silent for a few moments, then said, "Schmuck."

"I've got to get out of here."

Mike was sympathetic but couldn't actually do anything. I got off the phone. Shortly thereafter Dr. Mephistopheles and a few members of his staff appeared in the corridor. He said I could leave the psycho ward and advised me to pack my belongings. Evidently Dr. Korsten had leaned on him adequately.

While packing, it turned out that my Levi jacket was missing. The ward was searched but it couldn't be found. Then I found it scrunched up in a drawer of my cabinet. The thief evidently had returned it before the staff reached his room.

Dr. Mephistopheles unlocked the door to the psycho ward. It was a glorious feeling of freedom when I walked out into the next corridor, like escape from Alcatraz.

Dr. Mephistopheles said that he'd schedule psychotherapy for me, which is what he should have done in the first place. But instead, he wanted another subject for his psycho experiments after which he would write and publish a paper that would win him renown in the shrink community and perhaps a raise. The bastard used me when I was weakest and most defenseless, which led me to the obvious conclusion: not all shrinks are honorable people. They are susceptible to excessive ambition and money like everyone else.

I went home a new man. Somehow, I had survived

the basic snake pit experience. I realized clearly that I had to start fighting for my life. To hell with jumping out the window. To hell with suicide. Obviously, I needed to look at myself objectively and take action.

My most pressing problem was lack of funds. Fortunately, over the years I had renewed my hack license in case of emergencies. Clearly an emergency had befallen me. I took my hack license to a Manhattan taxi garage in the West 20s and they hired me on the spot.

So I became a cabdriver on the night shift again, 4pm to 4am, three nights per week, but it was better than the psycho ward. Anything was better than the psycho ward.

Every Wednesday afternoon for the next two years I rode a subway to the Bronx VA and sat for an hour with my newly assigned shrink, a lady in her forties who was a psychiatric nurse and proved to be absolutely fabulous.

She seemed to genuinely care about me and expressed sympathy for what had happened in the psycho ward. Then of course we explored my childhood, which she later described as "Dickensian". She always asked pertinent questions and her comments were right on. She seemed to have tremendous insights and understanding about the human condition and helped me understand myself and my predicament better. Psychotherapy works if you get a good therapist and you cooperate, no matter how painful it might be. Basically the patient dredges up pain, analyzes it with the aid of his shrink, and allows its wicked energy to dissipate.

Now my memory gets a little fuzzy. About six months after driving a cab, I vaguely remember visiting a former editor at the Harper publishing company. I don't remember who he or she was or what we talked about. As I was leaving, I ran into Ed Breslin near the elevators. He was a top executive at the company.

He asked, "How're you doing, Len?"

"I'm driving a cab these days."

His brow wrinkled. "You're too good a writer to be driving a cab. Call me tomorrow."

I called him. A new book contract was the miraculous result. I quit my cabdriving job and became an action/adventure writer again. My nightmare finally was over. And paradoxically I had to thank the psycho ward for my recovery because it forced me to realize that I didn't want to spend the rest of my life in psycho wards, and really didn't want to die, and must get my act together and fight for my life.

There are two morals to this story.

#1. Don't ever walk into an emergency room and say you're suicidal, because you'll lose all your rights as an American citizen and might become even more depressed and anxious than before you walked in.

#2. Don't ever voluntarily sign yourself into a psycho ward because it probably will worsen your condition.

I am not suicidal anymore. I've learned that I'm not inherently depressed with a chemical imbalance in my brain, but insufficient funds had the power to drive me crazy. Now I'm on Social Insecurity which pays my basic bills. I have become a happy camper, believe it or not.

I will close this long chapter with a pertinent quote from the great Anais Nin: "No one has described fully the horror of this illness called anxiety. Worse than any physical illness, this is an illness of the soul, for it is insidious, elusive and arouses no pity."

42

MY SECOND WESTERN SERIES

THE RESULT OF THAT CHANCE MEETING WITH ED BRESLIN was my second Western series. To get it rolling, first of all I had to write a presentation.

All my series began with the creation of a new main character or protagonist. So the question became: Who would he be this time?

Part of my creative process was and still consists of letting my mind wander while in my apartment or walking around outdoors or standing in the shower under hot jets. During one of those brainstorming sessions, my mind meandered back to 1953 when I was 18 and going through my first major life crisis.

The more I thought about my angst at age 18, the more I decided that my new protagonist would be 18 and have my exact confused, semi-immature but occasionally rational psychology, which I hoped would make the character believable, amusing, and a fully rounded character, not a John Wayne-type invincible Western hero who had few if any doubts about anything.

But my new character could not be me completely.

He needed to be more courageous, charismatic, attractive, tougher, heroic, more effective in the violence department, and possess all other qualities necessary for a Western hero or anti-hero protagonist. Yet he essentially was me with Billy Budd tossed into the mix.

So the big question becomes: who exactly was I at age 18?

I'm going to get into personal material here so that you'll get the full picture of who I was at age 18 and how *The Pecos Kid* developed out of me. This personal material might seem irrelevant but actually helped me formulate the multi-faceted in-depth personality of my new Western main character, because most of my qualities and attitudes would be transferred to him, warts and all.

I believe that all people are very complicated in different ways and each person is unique. So was I at age 18. Fundamentally I was a good-natured, easygoing teenager but also very messed up, living in public housing in New Bedford, Massachusetts, the city where I had been born in Saint Luke's Hospital.

Shortly before my above-mentioned major life crisis at age 18, I had been expelled from New Bedford Vocational High School for disrupting classrooms and interfering with other kids trying to learn. My specific transgressions consisted of class clown antics, distracting socializing foolishness, and avoidance of schoolwork by means necessary.

Around that time, I got in trouble with police because two of my buddies had a side gig of breaking into barrooms closed for the night and stealing cash plus everything portable that they could find. They gave me stolen booze and jewelry to hold for them, then got caught because basically they were young brainless baboons not much different from me. When detectives asked them about locations of stolen goods, my scared friends naturally gave them my name.

A short while later, I was home alone one afternoon, under the influence of stolen booze, wondering what to do about my screwed-up life, when there was a knock on the door. I opened up and there stood a heavyset middle-aged guy in a suit holding a badge before my very eyes. He informed me that my friends were in jail and had confessed that they gave me stolen goods. The detective then asked me to give him said loot.

I did not reply that I had no stolen goods. Instead, I had the presence of mind to lie that I didn't know stolen goods had been stolen. I went upstairs, gathered the swag and gave it all including unopened bottles of booze to the detective. He probably smelled my boozy breath but didn't arrest me. He just walked back to his car.

I felt certain that he would return and bust me. Perhaps I should get out of town? While wondering how to proceed, I had no idea that the worst was yet to come a few days later when I got into a big ugly argument with my drunken father, which became the aforementioned major life crisis.

Where was my mother? She died when I was four. The old villain who was my father dumped me into foster care, then took me back when I was nine. His method of dealing with me was straightforward physical intimidation. Yes, he smacked me around from time to time. I would be considered an abused child by today's standards, although I didn't feel like a victim and never felt sorry for myself that I can recall. I was living among low-income people not well educated. Domestic violence was not unusual but most of my neighbors generally were honorable and decent.

I was very stoical as a child and accepted my reality

as a problem that I just had to deal with as best I could. I disliked and feared the old son-of-a-bitch and often wondered if I really was his son. I knew that one day in the not-too-distant future I would be old enough to escape. Actually, I should have been grateful to him because he was teaching me valuable coping skills, which might have been his game all along.

Dear old Dad's physical intimidation couldn't go on forever because I was growing bigger as children inevitably do. On the evening in question, I was 18, taller and much better physically conditioned than he.

It also should be mentioned that I hung out a lot in the streets and learned that I absolutely could not allow anyone to push me around. It was considered better to lose a fight and get beaten to a pulp or even killed rather than get pushed around. I accepted those values without question as did every other male whom I knew in New Bedford.

I brought those values to the major life crisis which occurred shortly after the visit by the detective. The major life crisis was launched by another heated argument with dear old Dad. He always was insulting, criticizing and hassling me about one thing or another. I argued back and that evening must have really pissed him off. He was standing at the sink, washing dishes, and threw the dishrag at me.

It hit me in the face. I went apeshit and attacked him physically for the first time ever. He was in his fifties, drunk and out of shape whereas I was sober, young, in the best condition of my life. I won't go into gruesome details, because this little article is supposed to be about my second Western series, but suffice to say that I knocked him down twice and perhaps would have hurt him badly if our neighbor on the other side of the flimsy wall in the government housing project didn't hear everything, called our apartment on the telephone, and threatened to notify the police if we didn't stop fighting.

I was extremely agitated after the violence. Upstairs in my bedroom I wondered what in the hell to do next. It became increasingly clear that I was in deep trouble on all fronts and had better get out of town before my situation deteriorated further and I killed the old bastard or he killed me, or I went to jail as an accomplice to barroom burglaries.

Now I must digress again. Although a lousy high school student, I always read a lot and recently had finished reading a paperback novel called *Geraldine Bradshaw* by Calder Willingham, who was a big name on the literary scene in those days, now completely forgotten. The novel was about bellhops at a California resort hotel who had love affairs with movie stars, socialites and other beautiful women.

A plan formed in my immature overly-excitable mind. I decided to become a bellhop at a California resort hotel and have love affairs with movie stars, socialites and other beautiful women. I had accumulated some savings from my horrible boring supermarket job but didn't think enough was available to carry me all the way to California, so instead I'd go to Miami Beach, which I assumed was like California, and live my wonderful bellhop dream there.

I didn't sleep much that night because I thought the old rat would kill me while I was unconscious. Next day I went to Sears Roebuck, bought a cheap suitcase, stuffed it with some clothes, and hit the road.

That was back in 1953 when Jack Kerouac and Neal Cassidy also were on the road. They travelled in automobiles whereas I sat in a Trailways bus. Evidently, I was part of the Beat Generation without even knowing it.

In essence I was a teenaged vagabond on the face of the earth. I won't go into elaborate explanations about all that happened on the road, because again I'm supposed to be writing about my second Western series, but suffice to say that I met a few strange individuals on my journey, including a pretty blonde chick around my age with whom I became romantically involved on the bus and who wanted me to go with her to Spartanburg, South Carolina and work in a canning factory. Although severely tempted I continued to Miami, checked into the YMCA, and set out to become a bellhop and have love affairs with movie stars, socialites and other beautiful women.

Now back to New York City circa 1991. I decided that my new protagonist fundamentally would be me at age 18 on the loose in the Wild West instead of Miami Beach. Like me he thought he was capable of great achievements while uncomfortably aware that he actually was a dumb kid. Like me he would have tremendous confidence combined with monumental self-doubts. Like me he usually was an optimist although he had no good reason to be optimistic about anything. Like me he was very shy and awkward around girls unless they talked to him first.

Unlike me I conceived my new character as extraordinarily good-looking, more or less like Elvis Presley. Girls and even grown women went nuts over him, which confused and embarrassed him, while men would become jealous, causing him to get involved in violence which he could not avoid, and at which he became increasingly proficient. I don't remember exactly why, but my overheated imagination came up with the name "Duane Braddock".

What was his backstory? At this point my creative imagination kicked into overdrive. I decided that Duane Braddock had been orphaned as a baby and raised in a Roman Catholic Benedictine monastery in the Pecos region of Texas. His father was said to be an outlaw who got hanged, and his mother supposedly had been a prostitute who died shortly thereafter of some strange disease, although some said Duane's father had been a small rancher who lost a range war against big ranchers, and his mother had been a pious Catholic young lady who had married his father and died shortly after he was killed, after she gave birth to a little boy.

One day in the monastery Duane gets into a fight with another orphan and almost kills him. The old Abbot unceremoniously throws Duane out the gate. When the first novel in the series opens, Duane has just departed the monastery and is on a stagecoach headed toward a frontier town, as I left New Bedford after brawling with my father and was on a Trailways bus headed for Miami Beach.

Duane's immediate goal is to become a cowboy although he'd never ridden a horse, as my immediate goal was to become a bellhop although I knew nothing about the hotel business.

Duane's secondary goal is to find out the truth about his parents, as I often wondered about who was my real father. Duane's quest to discover more information about his parents partially drives plots of all novels in the series.

In that first small town Duane is befriended by an aging alcoholic gunfighter named Clyde Butterfield who teaches him the classic fast draw, as I met people in

Miami Beach who taught me about hotels and restaurants. Duane has very quick reflexes and becomes amazingly skilled with a gun, a huge advantage in the Wild West where many men with bad intentions are drunk and carrying guns.

He also falls in love with a saloon singer named Vanessa Fontaine known on the frontier saloon circuit as the Charleston Nightingale, a tall willowy blonde around five years older than he, based loosely on a model friend of mine who had appeared in *Vogue* and other fashion magazines. Vanessa falls in love with Duane against her better judgement, because he's so darned good-looking. She can't help herself, poor thing.

Naturally there are envious men who don't like Duane, such as the sugar daddy who loves and supports Vanessa financially. Naturally there are lots of outlaws and other nasty characters who decide to bully young Duane Braddock and come to regret it.

An unprincipled newspaperman sees Duane win a gunfight and decides to sell more newspapers by sensationalizing him as the notorious nefarious Pecos Kid. Duane's reputation as a gunfighter grows and naturally there are homicidal maniacs who want to make their reputations by killing him. He finally achieves his great ambition of becoming a cowboy, even lives with Apaches for a while, has many spectacular adventures while wandering the Wild West, gradually becoming more mature and learning more about his parents.

That was the premise for the series which I called *The Pecos Kid* by Jack Bodine. I wrote it up as a presentation; my literary agent Barbara Lowenstein sold it to Harper, thanks to Ed Breslin's encouragement. So I was back to work again, earning money and reliving my teenage years not in reality but as a cowboy in the Old West.

The series ran for six novels and wasn't renewed because of low sales or perhaps it also was considered an Adult Western at a time when Adult Westerns were going out of style, although there was no graphic pornography in *The Pecos Kid*.

I fell into economic distress yet again and needed to create another series immediately. What would it be this time? How could I dream up something all new again? Were my weary brain cells up to the task? For the answer to these and numerous other significant and meaningful questions, stay tuned.

You're probably wondering if I ever became a bellhop and actually had love affairs with movie stars, socialites and other beautiful women. The answer is a resounding no. After arriving in Miami Beach, I soon learned that bellhop jobs were highly prized, occupied by grown men with families, not dumb kids who just walked in off the sidewalk. So I became a dishwasher at a Kosher deli called Lechtner's on Espanola Way in what now is called South Beach, then became a busboy at the same deli, and finally a busboy at the Sea Isle Hotel at 30th Street and Collins Avenue, which in those days was a fairly new top-echelon Miami Beach joint.

Miami Beach pretty much closed down during the summer back then, so while there I interviewed for a busboy job at the Sagamore Hotel on Lake George in the Adirondack Mountains of upstate New York, got the job, and at the end of the Miami Beach season, travelled north in a driveaway car, worked as a busboy at the Sagamore, and was promoted to room service waiter.

Most waiters and busboys were college students on their summer breaks, earning money for their next school year. I was in awe of these college students who were knowledgeable about history, art, poetry, Shakespeare, science, etc. I wanted to be articulate and intelligent as they, but it wasn't a matter of simply mimicking them. I needed a piece to the puzzle but couldn't figure it out.

One of my best friends wasn't a college student, but a Mexican-American jazz trumpet player down on his luck, Chuck Vasquez. He'd taken a job as waiter at the Sagamore while his trumpet languished in a NYC pawnshop. Narrow waisted, handsome, with a black mustache, he was soft-spoken, no Spanish accent, and had been a frontline U.S. Marine in the South Pacific during World War II. Unlike that other combat veteran, my dear old Dad, Chuck was whimsical, never confrontational.

One afternoon I visited Chuck in his room, where he lay alone, clothed atop his bed, a strange-smelling cigarette between his fingers.

"What're you smoking?" I asked.

"Marijuana."

I was aghast, because I'd read about demon drugs. "But, Chuck – you've got to stop. It's bad for you."

"Not so bad," he said dreamily, and apparently wasn't suffering in the least. "Want some?"

"What does it do?"

"Kind of relaxes me."

By then I was receiving a "contact high", or assimilating the mood of the marijuana smoker. He held out the joint. I had never smoked a cigarette of any type before, but took an experimental puff, inhaling as he advised me. I don't remember coughing or becoming ill, just kept suckin' on that joint, and after a while felt a pleasant buzz. Hallucinating, I viewed my life from an entirely odd, blissful perspective. Lieutenant Lenny of the Space Cadet Corps finally had found rocket fuel. As I launched into the stratosphere, Chuck said, "Time to go to work."

I felt disoriented, my daydream turning into onerous chores. Chuck and I put on tuxedo pants, white shirts with black bowties, and red jackets with gold epaulets. Somehow, we arrived on the Sagamore veranda, where we stood side by side, backs to the wall, and stared into space, our round, brown bar trays flat on our hands. Fortunately, no customers disturbed our cannabis reveries.

I gazed at Lake George shimmering in the sunlight, surrounded by mountains like overturned bowls of green sugar. Feeling ecstatic, my jacked-up mind saw clearly that Mickey Mouse and Bugs Bunny were correct after all, life truly was a comedy, and I should relax more, instead of continually worrying.

Then a searing insight arrived like a thunderbolt from the hand of Zeus. If I wanted to be as smart as my college student friends, and become an upper-class person someday – why not simply go to college? This concept nearly bowled me over. I couldn't understand why I'd never thought of it before – it was so obvious.

Although stoned on weed, I knew that a college degree wouldn't be easy for a vocational high school throwout with no helpful parents to pay the bills. My drugged mind formulated an elaborate plan, as I stood like a zombie on the Sagamore veranda. I'd join the Army, which reputedly would accept anyone, even skinnybones like me. While in uniform, I'd finish high school via classes that the Army offered to ambitious soldiers. Following my discharge, if I didn't get killed in Korea, I'd attend college on the G.I. Bill. It seemed an eminently reasonable plan, and the crossroads of my life.

After returning to the planet Earth, I tested my plan

on college student friends, and all encouraged me, saying I was intelligent and could bring it off if I worked hard. On the radio, I heard that peace talks were underway between the U.S. and North Korean Communists, despite occasional provocations by the Communists. It seemed unlikely that I'd be killed in combat, so I swore solemnly to implement the plan. Whatever happened, nothing would prevent me from obtaining a college degree.

What drove this desire? I guess I felt inferior and needed a college degree to bolster my ego. Also, ambition was considered honorable in the 50s. For whatever reason, I was willing to endure any hardship, including three years in the Army and possible death by bayonet, to pursue knowledge and obtain a college degree.

I enlisted in the Army at the end of the summer hotel season, passed G.E.D. tests while stationed in Alaska, was awarded a high school diploma from the territory of Alaska, mustered out after three years active duty, attended Michigan State University on the G.I. Bill, and after graduation (class of 61) travelled to New York City to seek my fortune which I still haven't found and probably never will.

So that's the saga of my early years in a nutshell, and the story of *The Pecos Kid* series by Jack Bodine. The series has been republished as ebooks under my real name, Len Levinson, for anyone who might want to explore this peculiar matter in greater detail.

43

MY THIRD AND LAST WESTERN SERIES

My third and last Western series, published beginning in 1994, actually began long before I ever started typing it up.

It began during the early 1980s when my then girl-friend Marie and I were visiting her family in Tucson, Arizona. One warm summer day I was hiking alone in the vast Saguaro National Park, which once had been part of the Apache homeland. I carried sandwiches and two canteens of water in my backpack and wore a new cowboy hat purchased at Walmart.

Having spent most of my life on the East Coast, I never before experienced anything like the Sonoran Desert of Arizona. It seemed dazzlingly endlessly gorgeous. I discovered that the word "desert" does not mean 100% sand. Lots of cactus varieties and various bushes and trees grew on seemingly boundless tracts of shimmering terrain, with blue-gray mountains in the distance. I could see far away ethereal vistas. A family of wild pigs crossed my path that day.

After a while I felt tired, checked the vicinity for

rattlesnakes and sat in the shadow of a Cottonwood tree. No other human beings were visible so I smoked a cannabis cigarette as was my custom in those days.

Evidently, I went one or two tokes over the line because I became very ripped, which felt like a mild state of ecstasy. I could hear faint strains of the old Beatles song *Good Day Sunshine* echoing in my ears.

Then I started hallucinating. First, I saw colors and vague geometric shapes. The entire world felt like it was pulsating. My sense of time vanished, as if I were floating through eternity. Finally, I understood origins of the mysticism of the Carlos Castaneda/Don Juan books.

Then I saw them: a troop of cavalry advancing toward me, around twenty men in dusty blue uniforms and tan wide-brimmed hats, bearded, bleary eyed, exhausted, their horses' heads drooping down, returning from a long patrol through Apacheria.

They were led by a big burly officer with lieutenant's insignia on his shoulder straps. He was steady in his saddle, resolute, nobody to mess with, moving toward me across the sun-drenched desert. Behind him was a soldier carrying the guidon flag. Horses' hooves pounded the desert floor, sending up a cloud of dust.

They rode by and I thought: "Gee – someday I'd like to write a Western cavalry novel about that officer."

Fast forward to approximately 1993. I had just learned that the contract for my second Western series *The Pecos Kid* had not been renewed. I sank into deep melancholy because it felt like another rejection of me personally. I had poured my heart and soul into *The Pecos Kid* and thought it simply terrific. How could it possibly fail in the marketplace?

I could not sit around and cry in my carrot juice. I did not particularly feel like committing suicide. I needed to come up with another Western series fast, and hope that this new series would be more successful.

You probably know where this is going. I remembered that big burly cavalry officer and decided to build my new series around him.

At that point I'd written 77 published novels and was a very experienced novelist. As we all know, experience matters. I'd also done a huge amount of research on the Old West and American history in general. I decided it was time to elevate my game and really go for the gold.

My all-time favorite novel was and still is *War And Peace* by Leo Tolstoy. I decided that I would try to outdo Leo Tolstoy and write a huge sprawling series of interconnected novels in chronological order with many characters and situations, similar to how Tolstoy structured *War And Peace*. Tolstoy's background for his novel was the Napoleonic Wars and mine would be the Apache Wars.

This was an incredibly ambitious project, I know, I know. I thought I could handle it.

The Apache Wars began in 1846 when the United States Army marched into northern Mexico at the beginning of the Mexican War. The battleground encompassed the Apache homeland, a large section of which became part of the United States when the Mexican War ended in 1848. The Apache Wars continued until Geronimo surrendered in 1886. Apaches were the last American Indians to surrender. The war between Apaches and the U.S. Army was said to be the longest in American history.

I wanted my new series to be historical like *War And Peace* with many actual historical figures appearing on its pages. I also wanted to entertain my readers with American history as Tolstoy had entertained me with European history.

Like Tolstoy I wanted to write a fabulous magnificent meaningful saga that included, among other themes, characters trying to understand the meaning and purpose of human existence, plus the art and science of war, all within the context of a readable fast-paced action/adventure narrative. I wanted each novel to be 90,000 words which was substantially longer than my usual Western novels of 60,000 words each.

I called it *The Apache Wars Saga* by Frank Burleson and wrote an elaborate presentation. My literary agent Barbara Lowenstein had become busy with other projects, so assigned her assistant Nancy Yost to represent me. Nancy has since opened her own agency and become a high-profile literary agent but then she was just starting out in publishing. She sold *The Apache Wars Saga* to Signet. My first editor was Ed Stackler. The time finally had arrived for me to invest my many years of writing, reading and thinking into this series which I hoped would be the very pinnacle of my literary career.

The first novel in the series begins on the eve of the first major battle of the Mexican War, the Battle of Palo Alto which took place on the road to Matamoros. That big burly cavalry officer became Lieutenant Nathanial Barrington, graduate of West Point, son and grandson of Army officers, scion of a wealthy socialite New York City Whig family. As the novel opens, he is an aide-de-camp to General Zachary Taylor, known to the troops as "Old Rough and Ready", who is sitting at his desk inside his command post tent, planning tomorrow's action.

High up in the mountains, observing preparations for battle and later the battle itself is Mangas Coloradas, chief of the Mimbreno Apaches, accompanied by several of his foremost warriors. It is clear to them that a new military force is moving into their homeland and serious trouble lies ahead.

Thus the series begins. It will consist of many clashes, ambushes and all-out battles between American soldiers and Apaches, with Mexicans in the equation because northern Mexico also included a huge section of the Apache Homeland. Nathanial even marries a Mexican woman in the course of the series and has children with her.

I wanted to place the Apache Wars within the larger historical context of America during the stormy years leading to the Civil War. Characters in the series know that tensions are building throughout the land and even in the Army, like a deadly juggernaut locomotive speeding toward them, and no one can stop it.

The series includes in-person appearances by actual historical figures such as Abraham Lincoln, Jefferson Davis, Robert E. Lee, Ulysses S. Grant, Zachary Taylor, Stephen Douglas and Benjamin Louis Eulalie de Bonneville, among many others.

On the Apache side are: Mangas Coloradas, Victorio, Cochise, Geronimo and Cuchillo Negro, among many others.

I tried to present the war from both viewpoints. Neither side is depicted as the villain. I had read considerable anthropological material on Apaches and believed that I understood their culture and religion as well as a researcher could. I also returned to Arizona twice, and once visited the White Mountain Apache reservation near the Salt River Canyon.

There is love, hate, bloodshed, suspense, drama, shootouts, much true history and comparative religion in the series. I gave my best to it. The narrative is not dense and turgid despite my lofty Tolstoyan ambitions. I thought this series would blow the literary marketplace away and become a smashing critical and financial success.

It didn't. The contract was not renewed after #6. My last editor Todd Keithley, who had replaced Ed Stackler, told me: "They don't want little profits. They want *big* profits."

I replied, "But little profits add up to big profits."

He said, "They don't see it that way."

I was shattered by disappointment yet again. I couldn't understand how *The Apache Wars Saga* possibly could fail in the marketplace.

Although deeply disappointed, I didn't take it too personally because many action-adventure writers got dumped during the 1990s due to hot new policies implemented by rapidly conglomerating publishing houses. Advances usually paid to low profit writers like us got redirected to possibly profitable new authors, especially in the bestselling category, women's romances.

The last novel in the series #6 *Night Of The Cougar* published in 1997 closed down the narrative approximately in 1858. I had hoped to continue the series until the end of the Apache Wars in 1886. The cancellation crushed my plans.

I'll be very honest with you. I couldn't handle the failure of this series. Three of my standalone novels also had been rejected around that time. It appeared that my so-called literary career had crashed totally after 26 years and 83 published novels. My impression was that the publishing industry saw me as a loser and didn't want to have anything to do with me anymore.

I didn't see any point in writing something new if I couldn't sell it. I had very little savings. Somehow at the age of 62 I needed to go out into the world and find a job like a normal decent human being.

I ended up as a caseworker with the New York Administration for Children's Services where I worked for three years, 1997 to 2000 when I retired at 65 and finally returned to my so-called literary career.

The Apache Wars Saga by Frank Burleson has been republished as ebooks by Len Levinson, in case someone might be curious about this American version of *War And Peace* riding the range.

1. *Desert Hawks*
2. *War Eagles*
3. *Savage Frontier*
4. *White Apache*
5. *Devil Dance*
6. *Night Of The Cougar*

44

THE PECOS KID BECOMES A CASEWORKER

I NEVER PLANNED TO BECOME A CASEWORKER WITH THE New York City Administration for Children's Services (ACS). But in 1997, as discussed in the previous chapter, I went bust after writing 83 published paperback novels under 22 pseudonyms.

Desperately seeking income, I read employment ads and mailed resumes to private and government entities, but for a long while no human resources department showed a smidgeon of interest in a 62-year-old ship-wrecked novelist who hadn't held a real job for any appreciable amount of time in 27 years.

Then a letter arrived from ACS inviting me to an interview in lower Manhattan on April 29, 1997, for the position of caseworker. I satisfied the job requirement: bachelor's degree including 24 credits in the Social Sciences. No experience in child welfare necessary.

Actually I did have experience in child welfare. In 1968-69 I investigated child abuse/neglect for Dade County Youth Services in Florida. That bleak episode taught me that existence is catastrophic for certain children, and certain parents perhaps should be put before firing squads.

I also had worked for approximately six months in one of the adoption units of NYC's Child Welfare Administration circa 1993. (The Child Welfare Administration later changed its name to the Administration for Children's Services). All I did was fill out government forms, never saw a child and it was the most boring job I'd ever had but didn't give it much thought because soon I returned to writing novels.

They weren't exactly best-sellers so in 1997 I was prepping for my upcoming ACS interview by reading books and articles on child psychology and sociology. On interview day I dressed corporately and rode the A Train downtown.

I won't go into details of my hiring because this book is not about my caseworker career. I got the job as ACS caseworker and for three years dealt with children in foster care and their families in crisis.

I expected to find waste and inefficiency at this government agency but actually it far exceeded my expectations, to the detriment of children. It was difficult for me to accept that such a mess could be allowed to exist.

During my final ACS year, my frustrations became so all-encompassing, I decided to release them by writing a savage insider exposé newspaper or magazine-style article which I hoped would blow the lid off NYC child welfare, when and if it ever got published.

Every night for around three months I rode the subway home from ACS, sat at my computer and wrote until my eyelids wouldn't remain open. Then I collapsed into bed and prayed my effort would be published someday, to demonstrate to the world how government child-care created calamities for children.

After completing it, I consulted with literary friends about what publications might be interested. Several suggested the *Village Voice*. Jack Baxter, who wrote for the *Post*, called one of his friends at the *Voice*, Nat Hentoff, and recommended the article. Nat told Jack I should drop it off in the mailroom, care of Nat.

On May 18, 2000, I delivered the article to the Bowery offices of the *Voice*, confident it'd be tossed into the nearest trashcan because who cared about complaints from disgruntled government employees?

I turned 65 on May 20, 2000 and went on Social Insecurity. My last day on the job was Friday, May 27, 2000. Caseworker friends organized a retirement party in a meeting room at 150 William St. Many friends delivered speeches. Morris Heney, manager of my department, referred to me from the podium as "the conscience of ACS".

Afterwards I rode the subway back to my studio apartment in Hell's Kitchen, feeling like I'd just escaped from prison. Following a few days decompression, I returned to writing novels, and assumed my exposé lay moldering in a trash heap on Staten Island.

While writing a whodunnit called *Web Of Doom*, I received a call from Mr. Hentoff. He said he liked my article and would pass it to Don Forst, editor-in-chief of the *Voice*. According to my best recollection, I mumbled unintelligibly and nearly fainted.

A few days later, Don Forst called, said he wanted to publish the article and actually pay me for it. As close as I can remember, I became so emotional that I was unable to speak coherently.

The article ran as *Paper Purgatory* by Lenny Levinson

on June 20, 2000, the front-page story no less, with photo of *moi* inside wearing a white cowboy shirt. Many former ACS colleagues phoned and said they considered the article "great". Non-ACS friends I hadn't spoken with for years also praised the article.

I hoped *Paper Purgatory* would wake up politicians and the public about child welfare and inspire them to legislate significant reforms. Instead, following publication of the article, stories appeared in the New York press citing all the good work ACS was doing. No investigation of ACS was announced, my impassioned words caused no public commentary or improvements whatever, and *Paper Purgatory* disappeared into the dustbin of history along with my other failed literary endeavors.

A few days following publication, a caseworker friend phoned to report that Mr. Heney had said I was unwelcome in the ACS building at 150 William Street. Such was the fate of "the conscience of ACS".

45

MY GREAT AMERICAN CHILD WELFARE ARTICLE

IF YOU'D LIKE TO READ MY *VILLAGE VOICE* CHILD WELFARE article, here it is verbatim:

From the *Village Voice* June 20, 2000

PAPER PURGATORY
Inside New York's Foster Care System
by LENNY LEVINSON

First came an introduction by a *Village Voice* editor:

In 1997, 62-year-old Lenny Levinson was looking for work. After selling 83 paperback novels, mostly pulp adventure tales, he could no longer place his manuscripts. He landed a job as a caseworker at the Administration for Children's Services, from which he retired on May 26.

And here is my actual article as published:

As I write these words, I am crammed along with approximately 70 other individuals into an overheated waiting room on the fifth floor of Brooklyn Family Court. I am experiencing anxiety, because every sizable New York City public gathering contains at least one raving lunatic.

The one in this group is seated on a bench about 10 yards away. She is a well-dressed, heavyset, thirtyish black woman who is loudly denouncing the Hispanic male caseworker from the New York City Administration for Children's Services (ACS), who is sitting in the far corner, calmly reading the *Daily News*. According to the woman's tirade, the caseworker snatched away her children, alleging she was too mentally disturbed to care for them.

Is the mother merely angry, perhaps justifiably, or on the verge of violence? And what in the name of heaven or hell am I doing in this potentially hazardous situation? I am not a journalist or anthropologist, but an ACS caseworker from the Office of Contract Agency Case Management (OCACM). I am scheduled to attend a hearing concerning a child on my caseload whom I have never seen.

I had not planned to become an ACS caseworker. Until three years ago, I had been the undistinguished pseudonymous author of 83 paperback novels, most about cowboys and other tough guys seeking justice in an unjust world. But neither they nor my so-called serious novels were exactly bestsellers. No publishers demonstrated interest in my final three extravaganzas, and I was not deluged with job offers from Microsoft and Intel. Only ACS would hire a 62-year-old failed novelist.

The caseworker job requirement was a B.A. with 24

credits in psychology, sociology, or related social-science courses, which I accumulated during four years at Michigan State University, class of 1961. Despite the extreme age of these dubious credentials, plus my space-cadet mentality, I was hired by the New York City agency that serves foster children.

To prepare new hires such as myself for this important assignment, back when I began, ACS provided three weeks' training at its Satterwhite Academy in Jamaica, Queens. Most of the curriculum involved social theorizing, sensitivity training, and exercises during which participants wrote or drew cartoons with colored pens, like we did in kindergarten. My classmates and I were introduced to a gaggle of incomprehensible government forms and advised that we might occasionally be mandated to attend family court. The actual functioning of ACS never was explained coherently, and no one taught us how to perform our new jobs.

Which might explain my state of mind this morning in Brooklyn Family Court, where the same angry mother continues to rage against her caseworker. She hollers that she is on medication, but that doesn't make her a drug abuser or an incompetent parent. She spews vituperation, indignation, broken thoughts, pain and suffering, as she drags us through her psyche. Finally, a court officer takes her arm and gently leads her away. She does not resist, although she carries on her eloquent though disjointed tirade. In his corner, her caseworker continues to read the *News*.

I wonder what the notorious Pecos Kid, one of my favorite Western characters, would think of Brooklyn Family Court. No doubt he would simply shake his head, jump on his trusty horse, Tomahawk, and gallop away.

I calm myself by contemplating my upcoming court

appearance. I must testify on behalf of a four-year-old boy who recently was returned to foster care following an unsupervised weekend home visit with his putative birth father. The child allegedly reported to his maternal aunt/foster mother that his father had struck him so hard, he (the child) was knocked to the floor. The child also made the same statement to an investigator from the ACS Office of Confidential Investigations (OCI). But the child showed no marks, and no eyewitnesses can corroborate the child's story.

I never met the child, birth mother, or putative birth father. No valid reason exists why I should be in court, since I know only the child's paperwork, and can contribute no firsthand testimony. But ACS procedures have mandated my appearance, as they mandate substantial other unproductive activities.

Meanwhile, on another bench, a female teenager sucks her thumb while caressing her nose, like an infant. Around us swirl confusion, frustration, recrimination, shrieking children, and families coping with monumental issues. Fluorescent light throws ghastly rays on dirty blue-and-yellow walls. Ceiling tiles have been stained by water leakage. The government wall clock never deviates from one minute to two.

This is the real-deal world of children's services today, a descendant of the child-welfare state inaugurated during the Great Depression in Franklin Delano Roosevelt's first administration. To fight poverty, President Roosevelt and his brain trust devised numerous government programs. One was named Aid to Dependent Children (ADC), which mailed checks to citizens then known as "unwed mothers". ADC continues to provide money and services to children of what now are termed "single parents". The percentage of children born to single parents has increased approximately fivefold since ADC began in 1935.

What's the connection between Aid to Dependent Children and abuse or neglect? I have read records of approximately 250 children adjudicated abused/neglected, and I estimate that 95 percent were raised on Aid to Dependent Children or other public assistance programs. ACS currently has 34,000 children in foster care. The national foster-care population is roughly 546,000 children.

According to records I have read, the abuse and neglect children have suffered includes beatings that resulted in broken bones and lacerations, plus burns, torture, insufficient nourishment, medical neglect in which mothers do not take sick children to free clinics, and educational neglect in which mothers do not send children to free schools. Some children are born with birth defects due to lack of prenatal care, despite availability of free clinics and hospitals. Other children are born HIV-positive or addicted to cocaine. Many children are voluntarily placed in government foster care by parents who can't cope with their own flesh and blood.

Most of the children on my caseload are angry, perhaps because they feel cheated out of a decent life. They suffer pain and low self-esteem, often because they know that their absentee fathers don't give a damn about them, and their mothers are too busy with outside activities, such as smoking crack. Conventional psychological and social worker theories have failed most of these children. Nothing makes an impression except Ritalin.

Of course, not all foster children are disturbed. Some not only survive foster care but even graduate from college, a testimony to their sterling inner qualities and the skills of some foster mothers. These rare success stories are paraded periodically before TV cameras, but of my approximately 50 teenagers of college age to date, only three have gone to college and none have graduated. By my count, 80 percent of my teenaged foster children are doing poorly in school—and acting out big time.

Sometimes, after hours of reading case records, I want to scream or cry. I wake up in the middle of the night, thinking about these children. I sincerely want to help them. Instead, I fill out government forms.

According to my job description, I "monitor" two nongovernment welfare agencies, Episcopal Social Services and Graham-Windham, both contracted by the city to provide homes and services to the 126 foster children on my caseload. Translated from officialese, "monitoring" means reading reports written by contract-agency social workers and signing my name at the bottom, then filling out innumerable government forms based on information in the reports. I have no idea if these reports are accurate, and apparently it doesn't matter. I must sign anyway.

Instead of regularly visiting children for whom I am legally responsible and seeing the truth with my own eyes, I do paperwork. The reason is simple: If the paperwork isn't completed, the city loses federal funds. The more government forms completed, the more federal money the city receives.

Most of the paperwork is ludicrously redundant. For example, consider Form RES 1A, which I must fill out every six months for each child. This form can require a half hour or more to prepare, because necessary data may be lacking. After digging up obscure details and filling in blanks, I submit Form RES 1A to my supervisor, who signs off, and Form RES 1A goes into the family's case record, where it serves no purpose that I can determine.

The bureaucratic rationale for Form RES 1A is that it certifies that the child still is in foster care, but why should someone think that the child has left foster care, since the child never has been discharged? I have racked my brain and consulted with three supervisors, but we can discover no reason for Form RES 1A. Perhaps while I sleep at night, a lobster-shift supervisor accesses my files and studies my Forms RES 1A for a secret government initiative.

And then there's Form 2970, on which I also must certify that a child is in care, although the child never has left care—or in other words, duplication of pointless effort at taxpayer expense.

For another ludicrously redundant example, consider the court Extension of Placement Petition, whose purpose is simply to get on the docket and provide basic facts to the judge. One or two pages would suffice, but instead, for one child, a caseworker is required to fill in the blanks of a 16-page government document. If four children are on the case, not unusual, the caseworker will wind up with 64 pages. Each page must be photo-copied as many as 10 times, as must other documents containing pertinent information that first must be typed or written into the petition package. No bureau-crat has explained why pertinent documents can't be submitted without their contents being rewritten, but bureaucratic appetites for superfluous documentation are bottomless. When completed, the petition package will contain over 2600 pages for four children, and another tree has been chopped down in Maine.

For one child, the birth mother's name must be written or typed in seven different places (in the same petition package!), the child's name in six, the docket number in five, the child's birth date in five, the case ID number in six, the child's ID number in two, the date of removal in two, the date of original adjudication in two, the agency worker's name in three, and the caseworker's in five. Naturally, none of this repetitious clerical labor helps foster children.

The Extension of Placement Petition was designed by a staff headed by ACS deputy general counsel Joseph Cardieri, appointed by Mayor Rudolph Giuliani. The city loses federal funds when petitions are filed late, which occurs, I have been told, about 7 percent of the time. Ergo, one would expect Cardieri to streamline the petition-filing process. But ACS bureaucrats lack the capacity to recognize and remove obstacles, while the taxpayers' only function is to foot the bill.

Whenever a problem is identified or imagined by ACS management, a new government form is designed. At least five new forms have been introduced since I began employment, and there's no end in sight. We have government forms that track other government forms! The same information is written or typed again and again, and signed by numerous layers of bureaucracy, wasting time and resources.

No matter how hard I try, I simply cannot get on top of my paperwork, and in addition I must languish at court, or travel to the far reaches of the city, such as the last stop of the A train on Lefferts Boulevard in Queens, for conferences with children who generally don't arrive. I am mandated to participate in a planning review for each of my children every six months. This is a superficial encounter by any reasonable standard, especially since the parents or children seldom show up for the appointments.

Today in Brooklyn Family Court I sit on the floor, back against a wall, cross-legged like an Apache, because the benches are filled to overflowing. The waiting room has been cleverly designed without windows and ventilated by soot-covered overhead shafts. In the Old West, even jails had windows so a horse thief could see a ray of daylight to soothe his troubled soul, before the final sashay to the hangman's noose. This waiting room also offers views of the men's and women's lavatories, with doors open and toilets flushing.

A uniformed court officer saunters in and declares, "If you've got a case in part three—please check in!" A human mass gathers like cattle around the court officer, blocking the door and elevators beyond, so no one can enter or depart the waiting room. The din reaches astonishing loudness, with no knob to turn it down.

After checking in, clients and caseworkers return to benches. Then court officers call names, and people shuffle to courtrooms in other regions of the court building, where behind closed doors, well-intentioned overworked judges determine fates of families based on hasty and intimidating courtroom interviews augmented by government forms completed by ill-informed caseworkers such as me.

A hassled male attorney in his late twenties, from the Division of Legal Services (DLS), approaches me and says, "We haven't been able to service the father, so I don't know what's going to happen. Maybe I'll try to get the case adjourned." He walks away.

I return to my seat on the floor and read an essay written in 1712 by Sir Richard Steele, a favorite author of George Washington and Thomas Jefferson: "All Strictness of Behavior is so unmercifully laughed at in our

Age, that the other much worse Extreme is the more common Folly."

The rebellion against strictness of behavior has made deep inroads at ACS. Thanks to the Social Services Employees Union (SSEU), ACS caseworkers usually are not dismissed except for egregiously terrible behavior, such as the caseworker who urinated on his desk approximately five years ago, or the caseworker who kept his job though he did virtually no work. One day the latter caseworker's supervisor asked the caseworker to complete at least one task to justify his salary, whereupon the caseworker threatened the supervisor with bodily harm. Shortly thereafter, the caseworker was fired. The moral here is: Don't threaten your supervisor and don't urinate on furniture.

Despite these vagaries, most of my fellow caseworkers and supervisors are hardworking human beings who care about children and want to improve their lives. The main barrier is an aloof management apparatus strong on public relations and paperwork, but little else. Morale among the rank and file is rock-bottom, and caseworker turnover is constant, resulting in discontinuity of child care.

Around 10 a.m., the contract-agency social worker on my case arrives, waves wearily, and squeezes onto a bench at the far edge of the waiting room, where she removes paperwork from her briefcase and proceeds to write. I have dealt with her before. In her late twenties, she is bright, dedicated, and burning out at an alarming rate. Perhaps she was up half the night because of a foster child in a police station, a not uncommon circumstance for foster children and agency social workers.

Approximately 90 percent of my foster children manifest behavior known as "oppositional" in the trade.

About 40 percent of my foster children become chronic truants, chronic runaways, criminals, street fighters, and/or single mothers while in the care and custody of the commissioner of ACS, Nicholas Scoppetta, a lawyer appointed by Mayor Giuliani.

Virtually all ACS caseworkers and supervisors who have expressed themselves regarding Commissioner Scoppetta in my presence think he hasn't a clue about what's happening in the agency he heads. Commissioner Scoppetta is a former foster child himself; therefore, it is assumed he understands these children's needs. Many caseworkers, including me, also have been foster children, but regardless of our family backgrounds, caseworkers generally agree that Commissioner Scoppetta's hands-off, papercentric management style undermines the well-being of foster children.

I have seen the lordly Commissioner Scoppetta twice during my employment. The first encounter was January 14, 1999, at a lecture/training session concerning the recently enacted Adoption and Safe Families Act (ASFA). Hundreds of caseworkers packed the historic Great Hall at Cooper Union, where we were mandated to hear the commissioner's courtroom delivery. He is a skilled television performer, I'm told.

My second sighting of Commissioner Scoppetta occurred a few months later in the dreary box canyons of 150 William Street. The well-tailored jurist rushed down a corridor, surrounded by his praetorian staff, and he did not acknowledge the existence of caseworkers in the vicinity. Commissioner Scoppetta diligently avoids interaction with caseworkers who might talk straight to him and perhaps awaken him from his slumber.

I have heard caseworkers say, "ACS is designed to

fail." My theory is that ACS never was designed at all, but sort of grew into the current dysfunctional monstrosity.

Child welfare in New York City began officially in 1832 when laws regulating the treatment of children were passed by city government. In 1895, the city elected to deliver services through private charitable institutions, known as contract agencies. As a result, New York City foster care today consists of two entirely separate, miscommunicating, and constantly warring entities. One is the city-controlled ACS itself, a leaky, rudderless barge floating on a swamp of paper-work. The other comprises approximately 60 private foster agencies funded by tax dollars, and allegedly monitored by ACS, but in practice they operate as loose cannons on the deck of the aforementioned sinking barge.

Although there is a tendency to trace the root of every social evil to insufficient government funding, money is not the main problem with ACS. The total ACS budget is $2.1 billion annually. With around 34,000 children in foster care, it computes to a staggering $61,764 per child!

Why does New York City foster care cost more than a year at Harvard, Yale, or Princeton? Let's follow the money trail. First, an ACS field-office caseworker on government payroll is assigned to investigate a report to the state of child abuse/neglect. If the case is "indicated," the child might enter foster care, and might be placed in a contract-agency foster boarding home or group home funded by tax dollars, but with minimal government oversight. The child then is assigned one agency social worker, who is mandated to see him/her once every two months, according to minimum standards. The agency social worker is backed up by a supervisor, the agency's assistant director and director, plus support staff and psychologists.

In addition, each foster child soon lands on the caseload of an ACS caseworker such as me, plus supervisor I, supervisor II, supervisor III, deputy manager, manager, deputy director, director, deputy commissioner, commissioner, DLS lawyers and judges, support staff, plus numerous executive-type people, including certain individuals possessing advanced social-work degrees who attend international conferences, or develop new government forms, or modify government forms already in use, or monitor caseworkers who monitor private agencies who monitor children. ACS employs roughly 8000 individuals, all requiring office space in one of the most overpriced real estate markets on the planet Earth.

Despite this multitude of government and contract-agency employees, and the annual expenditure of $61,764 per child, each child is seen only once a month by one agency social worker, and once every six months (maybe) by one ACS caseworker, in addition to receiving basic food, shelter, clothing, medical care, and an allowance (for kids over 14), according to minimum standards. You don't need an MBA to know that a huge chunk of tax dollars is devoted to bureaucracy, not children.

I have spoken with at least 40 contract-agency social workers, and they all said that they needed more visits with each child, but couldn't manage it due to over-whelming caseloads and high volumes of paperwork. One social worker explained that she could handle 15 children effectively, making certain they receive what-ever they need to thrive, in addition to interviewing parents, appearing in court, and the usual filling out of paperwork. Instead she's got 32 children, all of whom need help, but must wait for services, during which time they may disrupt classrooms, punch people, join gangs, become runaways, sell drugs, get arrested, become pregnant, or go berserk. This is no exaggeration. Foster children are a wild bunch, and by the time help arrives, it's usually too little too late.

What's the answer? First, jettison the private agencies but incorporate their foster homes into ACS and hire their social workers and supervisors. Then provide one ACS caseworker, one supervisor, and one manager for one child, with one weekly visit from the caseworker, one monthly visit from the supervisor, and one two-monthly visit from the manager, supported by a trimmed-down childcentric ACS management staff. Dump ludicrous paperwork, and assign ACS's nonproductive staffers to actual child care. These reforms would approximately double the number of frontline caseworkers available to help troubled foster children.

The cost of these reforms would not exceed the present budget, since all the above already are on the government payroll. If more frontline caseworkers were available, they could spend more time assessing needs of the children and developing remedies that could be implemented more quickly. If foster children received more rapid interventions, they might lead happier lives.

A chilling statistic I've heard often cited at ACS: More than 70 percent of NYC's homeless are graduates of city foster care. This is one colossal failure that cries for reform, but ACS's management can be as misguided as it pleases, because the public at large is not well informed about its operations.

Only an ACS insider would know that my previous director, Robert Pearlman, retired about two years ago and accepted the position of director of social services at the Catholic Guardian Society, a private contract agency. What's wrong with that? Perhaps private contract agencies exist to provide employment for retired ACS management executives. Or maybe private agencies help dilute responsibility in lawsuits against the city. Or possibly ACS management prefers to deal with nonunion private agencies rather than the militant and often unreasonable Social Services Employees Union. I can think of no other excuses for this two-headed, arthritic abomination.

Meanwhile, back in Brooklyn Family Court, my agency social worker colleague advises me that my child client has arrived, accompanied by his government-subsidized foster mother, who also is the child's maternal aunt. I drop to one knee in front of my clean, healthy-appearing child client and gaze into his eyes for the first time. I ask how he's doing. He does not respond, refusing to acknowledge my existence, and instead plays with his three cousins, whom his maternal aunt/foster mother brought to court. The child's reaction is understandable; I'm a complete stranger, although I will be making determinations affecting the rest of his life.

I initiate conversation with the maternal aunt/foster mother. She admits she's never liked the putative birth father and always considered him dangerous.

"Why'd your sister get involved with him?" I ask.

She shrugs, reluctant to say more, perhaps due to fear of the birth father. Or possibly she fears me, because a caseworker can snatch people's children, or help clients obtain government housing, or terminate government checks.

I return to my seat on the floor, where I update progress notes concerning my case. A female teenager looks at me and says to her male teenager companion, "Watch out for that guy over there."

I wait for my DLS attorney to return. Although DLS attorneys are the stars of Brooklyn Family Court, you have to wonder why they would accept the low pay and high pressure of their jobs. Perhaps they are social workers at heart, or they rejected corporate America's merciless competition, or corporate America rejected them. One DLS attorney said that he didn't feel comfortable defending murderers in criminal court.

Some DLS attorneys present themselves as Ally McBeals in high-fashion miniskirts and suit jackets. Others dress as college professors, oddball bohemians, Las Vegas lounge lizards, or aging hippies. My attorney favors the natty Wall Street look, plus hiking boots, and is unquestionably intelligent, committed, and frazzled. When he finally returns, he tells me, "I'll ask for substitute service, consolidate both cases, and adjourn."

"When can I return to my office?"

"I have seven more cases. We'll see."

Here are the basics of the case facing me: The birth mother and putative birth father had a romance that produced our child client. The birth mother has been and still might be a crack smoker, and she previously experienced other romances, which produced three other children from two or more unnamed birth fathers. The birth mother has demonstrated little interest in any of her children, each of whom is in foster care due to abuse/neglect, and all are displaying behavioral difficulties, including armed robbery by the oldest son (age 13), despite social worker counseling and psychological evaluations. The birth mother told the social worker that if the government terminates her parental rights, "I'll just make more babies."

The putative birth father is employed as a handyman in a Manhattan office building and has petitioned the court for custody of his son. He resides alone in a Bronx apartment full of used television sets, VCRs, piles of electrical cables, and possibly propane gas tanks. According to the social worker, the birth father still loves the birth mother, who apparently no longer cares for him. The birth father believes the birth mother's family is poisoning his son's mind against him and indoctrinating the child with physical-abuse scenarios. It is impossible to know who's telling the truth.

After spending most of the day in Brooklyn Family Court and never appearing before a judge, I get released by my DLS lawyer. I ride the subway back to my lower Manhattan cubicle, where I find a new mountain of paperwork waiting.

When I began as an ACS caseworker, I expected government waste to confirm my worst suspicions. I have found government waste far exceeding my worst suspicions, to the detriment of children. After more than 50 years of varied employment, I have never worked for such incompetent executives.

I recently reached retirement age, and rode off into the sunset like a graybearded old cowpoke. But what about the children I have left behind? What chance will they have to survive ACS foster care? And how much social damage will these children inflict, thanks to irresponsible parenting combined with rank ineptitude at ACS?

It's not about more funding, the usual focus of the phoney-baloney public-policy debate. It's about the will to change, and the banality of evil.

MY GREAT AMERICAN CHILD
WELFARE BOOK

IN THE YEAR 2000, AFTER THREE YEARS AS CASEWORKER with the New York City Administration for Children's Services (ACS), I turned 65, went on Social Insecurity and returned to my so-called literary career.

I was and remain a habitual reader of news and became increasingly annoyed by discrepancies between glowing media reports of ACS and it's actual extreme dysfunction witnessed in person from within by me. Finally I got so mad I decided to write a book about my experiences in child welfare, in the perhaps hopeless hope that a civic-minded publishing company might take it on, and American taxpayers might learn how their tax dollars were being wasted in the name of compassion, aided and abetted by hypocrisy, resulting in tremendous suffering for children.

To cut to the chase, two versions of this book were rejected by several houses. So I re-wrote it. And re-wrote it. To this day it has not been published.

Why was I so obsessed about ACS dysfunction? Why

couldn't I move on like a normal, healthy-minded, well-adjusted individual?

Perhaps it's time to 'fess up. I had a major conflict of interest. As touched on briefly before, I'm a former foster child myself.

Often while reading cases or meeting foster children, I experienced flashbacks of my own throwaway childhood. Mother died when I was four and dear old dad tossed me into foster care because he couldn't cope. I resided in a series of foster homes in the vicinity of Boston, Massachusetts for five years.

I understand how immature minds can feel while adrift in an incomprehensible foster system. I don't recall seeing one social worker after my initial processing. My various foster parents were neglectful rather than abusive, caring little about me and other foster kids, while receiving checks to care for us. Dear old dad visited me exactly three times during the five years I was in foster care.

He took me back when I was nine but turned out to be a violent alcoholic so I too was an abused/neglected child. His discipline consisted of threats of physical violence and actual physical violence. Once he smacked me in the face with a shredded belt, so I know how it feels to reside with an ignorant, vicious, alcoholic parent. When I became an adult, I learned from my mother's cousins that he also beat on my mother occasionally. What a great guy.

Somehow I survived childhood. I cannot say why definitively. One possible reason was that I knew someday I'd grow up and escape dear old dad, which actually happened when I was 18. Another possible reason is that I've always been and still remain stoical, which provides strength and stability when under pressure.

As a child, I wasn't especially fearful of physical violence because no permanent damage ever was done, pain vanishing after a day or two. Some kids are resilient. Others crack easily. Why?

Psychologists generally believe our fundamental personalities are formed during our first four years. I spent those years with a loving, intelligent mother. So I owe everything to her, although barely remembering her.

47

MY LITERARY CAREER COMES
TO AN ABRUPT HALT

AFTER COMPLETING MY GREAT UNPUBLISHED CHILD welfare non-fiction book, I returned to my fiction-writing career. I had three completed unpublished standalone novels on my hard disk and decided to polish them to a high level of perfection and sell them for big bucks.

What about income while working on these three standalone novels? Social Security checks were deposited regularly in my checking account, which covered my basic expenses, and I had a weekend job as doorman and security guard in a building across the street from the Trump Tower. For this job I wore a uniform that made me look like an admiral in the Czar's Imperial Navy.

Everything was going well, I felt happy and well-adjusted, making good progress on my various writing projects, when I was hit with the equivalence of a hydrogen bomb. During a routine medical check-up, I was diagnosed with advanced prostate cancer. I decided on the surgery option over radiation. My daughter

Debbie had relocated to the Chicago suburbs, and I thought it might be wise to have surgery in her vicinity, so she could help me during recovery. She agreed.

I underwent what is called Radical Retropubic Prostatectomy at the University of Chicago Hospital. My urologist and surgeon was Dr. Charles Brendler. How do I deal with crises? I write about them. Here is the article I wrote about my prostate cancer:

NO MORE ERECTIONS
a true life sex story
by Len Levinson

PART ONE

A few hours following prostate cancer surgery (on 1/25/2001), as I lay stoned on Demerol in my hospital bed, my urologist in pale, green scrubs delivered bad news. Cancer had grown out of my prostate gland into surrounding tissue, necessitating removal of my prostate gland, lymph nodes and the nerve bundle that produced erections. My cancer apparently was eliminated and my life saved but the subtext of his message was my sex life as I knew it was over.

This verdict didn't bother me much at the time thanks to Demerol. If the urologist wanted to lop off my head – be my guest. Who needed erections or a head as long as I had Demerol?

During convalescence, reality set in. I was 65, unmarried and latest blood tests confirmed that I'd survived prostate cancer *but* my greatest all-time pleasure was over, finito, terminated by a flick of the surgeon's wrist.

I struggled to accommodate my new reality. Penis-oriented intercourse with naked women in bed had been the primary focus of my life prior to prostate cancer surgery. Whenever I walked into a room, whether corporate suite, museum gallery or funeral parlor, the first thing I did was check out the women. Now the party was over although the lights hadn't gone out.

What was the point of living without carnal love? It was penis envy in its purest form. I didn't feel like a 100% man anymore.

Although tempted, I didn't commit suicide. Because in addition to being a sex maniac, I also was a half-baked intellectual. And I found myself wondering what exactly was a man anyway?

Was it courage that made a man? No because many women have demonstrated courage in battle, like Joan of Arc. Was it sheer physical strength? No because women weightlifters and other athletes were far stronger than I at age 65. Was it aggressiveness? No because many women of my acquaintance, and certainly my literary agent, were far more aggressive than I ever dreamed of being. It seemed that women could equal men in all areas except one. Women couldn't get erections. Therefore a man is a creature who gets erections.

Ergo, I wasn't a man anymore. Thanks to post-modern surgical science I'd become some kind of neutered hound dog, or sexless cyborg or postmodern eunuch.

Eighteen days after surgery, my urologist and I had a long talk. He said I was cancer free based on new blood tests. Viagra wouldn't help but all wasn't lost. I could utilize a hydraulic pump to draw blood into my penis, then clamp on a ring to prevent blood from escaping back to mainline arteries. Or I could jab a hypodermic needle into my penis, then inject a chemical that produced erections. Or I could insert a syringe into my urethra and squeeze in another chemical. These solutions seemed totally horrible and completely disgusting.

My sex life seemed moot anyway because I was mostly immobilized, recuperating with my daughter Debbie and her husband Dan in Aurora, Illinois, a Chicago suburb.

Debbie and Dan worked during the day, ideal because I required solitude to think through no more erections. But the more I thought, the more I found no remedy. Because no secondary, non-penis activity could hope to compete with the main event, at least for me. I must adjust to my new neutered condition, pointless to search for absent answers.

To distract myself I tried cable television but became even more depressed after a week of watching lady newscasters, movie queens, dancers, etc.

So I decided to read something. As student and occasional practitioner of various religions, with plenty of time on my hands, I selected the entire Bible, both Old Testament and New, my goal to read it front to back like a history volume or mythical extravaganza.

I thought it might be tedious, but the Good Book was lean, crisp writing drawing me into a vast Technicolor epic packed with blood-soaked wars, incredible catastrophes, sublime poetics and profound wisdom, altogether offering a more comprehensive vision of existence. My personal suffering seemed relatively minor compared to Job afflicted with boils from head to foot, his children killed in a hurricane, or Sodom and Gomorrah demolished, or Jesus crucified.

But when I looked out the window and observed pretty women strolling about, desperation returned. I didn't think I could continue without them, despite the Good Book.

I quit looking out the window but couldn't hide from the world. After six weeks with Debbie and Dan I returned to my apartment on West 55th Street near Ninth Avenue in Hell's Kitchen, midtown Manhattan. Among my first duties was appearing before my New York urologist. Additional blood work verified that prostate cancer still was absent. Time to get on with my life.

Over the years I'd evolved into a relatively unsuccessful pulp fiction novelist. So I continued writing several hours per day in my rent-stabilized Hell's Kitchen apartment, but difficulties presented themselves when I needed supplies or fresh air.

As is well-known and thoroughly documented, magnificent women from everywhere emigrate to the Big Apple to become models, actresses, dancers, singers, lawyers, journalists, medical students, social workers, literary agents, etc. I passed them on sidewalks, in supermarkets, at the Barnes and Noble, in museums or Central Park. I knew that I'd never get down with any of them ever again, and it took the heart right out of me.

But I wasn't totally deluded. Pre-surgery I probably wouldn't enjoy love affairs with those ravishing ladies either. But the remote possibility of success always had been available. After all, in the past I'd participated in and suffered through love affairs with women I'd considered beautiful. "The no's don't count – only the yes's count," said a great Brooklyn Lothario of my acquaintance.

Then I noticed a new, peculiar phenomenon. Women attracted me in my mind, but no sensuality or eroticism manifested in my body, only unpleasant twinges in my lower abdomen. After much self-monitoring, I concluded that erotic sensations and feelings evidently had been part and parcel of erections. All seemed located on the same neurobiological circuit based on my personal experience, not an article in a medical journal. If that specialized nerve bundle was removed –goodbye erotic sensations and feelings in Lenny.

For example, if I spotted a semi-naked, eighteen-year-old stunner on the sidewalk, gliding along on roller blades, certain lurid thoughts automatically erupted into my mind. Under normal circumstances those thoughts transmitted a biochemical-electrical impulse addressed to my nerve bundle that produced erections. Soon I'd feel overheated, half-crazed, not unlike the Marquis de Sade prowling the back streets of Marseilles, searching for action.

Minus my erectile nerve bundle I felt numb or dead inside, not fully human, the new Bionic Lenny. Sometimes when glancing at a particularly significant female I reflected that I might be better off if I'd simply died of cancer.

One evening I dined with my literary agent. She asked how I was getting along after surgery. I explained some of the above, omitting darker speculations because I didn't want to depress her. She suggested I write a hands-on, consumer information article about intercourse assisted by hydraulic pumps, hypodermic needles and syringes.

But I wasn't married or living with a woman with whom to conduct educational experiments. Even if I managed to undertake romance with a new significant other, I couldn't imagine, at a tender moment, dragging a hydraulic pump from beneath the sofa and saying, "Ever see one of these?"

Mental health professionals generally believe that gloomy thoughts are unproductive. Through trial and error, I discovered that it wasn't difficult to divert my attention from delectable females to other sights. I merely glanced away at New York City architecture or a novel on sale in the Strand Book Store window or a street peddler's table. In essence I was conditioning myself like a laboratory rat.

I discussed some of these matters with another woman friend who wasn't an ex-lover; we'd never been mutually attracted romantically. Like my literary agent she also suggested I try pumps and other implements but incorporate a sense of humor. She pointed out that sex sometimes was funny.

Sex never was comedy for me. I had considered it absolutely necessary for mental and physical well-being, like air I breathed and water I drank. Sometimes in the toils of passion I had even uttered exaggerated declarations of love to my paramour of the moment.

As newly-minted eunuch I admitted that I'd behaved dishonorably with certain of them, while they tore my heart to shreds. From my new post-surgical perspective, prostate cancer appeared a blessing in disguise, transforming me into a decent human being in spite of myself.

Another woman friend suggested that men and women could participate in varieties of sexual behavior outside the format requiring erections. Again, I explained that I didn't have normal erotic feelings, only freaky lower abdominal soreness when provoked. But I knew precisely what she meant, the little vixen.

At another meeting with my literary agent, she said, "I think it's all in your mind." In other words, she implied not-so-subtly that my sexual crisis was merely another symptom of my neuroses, as if surgical destruction of my sex life was no big deal. Or perhaps she was informing me indirectly that I'd crossed the line into obsession.

The laboratory rat worked intensively to condition himself. After a few months my sexual dysfunction seemed under control. But I only conned myself yet again. For example, I might be wandering midtown Manhattan, contemplating whether to check latest CDs at Virgin Records, or the new exhibit at the Museum of Modern Art, when a voluptuary in thin summer dress sashayed within range, and I became the human equivalent of a battleship struck by a nuclear torpedo. Often I thought a bottle of sleeping pills might be my ideal solution.

But if I destroyed myself, I couldn't travel the U.S.A. and visit my children and grandchildren. And I couldn't shoot the breeze with friends, attend opera, ballet, concerts, movies, plays or read great novels or dine in Chinese, Mexican and Italian restaurants. And I couldn't write towering novels and essays no publisher wanted to print.

I worked to convince myself that sexuality wasn't 100% of existence. I should be grateful for the opportunity to enjoy women as human beings, not just as sexual gratification machines. Stop complaining and move on already.

This became my eminently practical and seemingly necessary intellectual framework for Eunuchville. But mind games often are shot off their perches by the rifles of reality. An unimaginable encounter was on my agenda to complicate profoundly my already tangled conundrum of no more erections.

PART TWO

No rational person would admit what I'm going to admit right now, but in the interests of medical research, or for students of Abnormal Psychology – I'm going to tell it like it is. Because I'll bet that many highly proficient urologists, oncologists and psychologists have no idea what can happen to a man who loses, during surgery, his nerve bundle that makes erections, yet retains his life if you can call no more erections living.

The misadventure began innocently enough in Central Park around 18 months following surgery. I was circling The Lake on my usual late afternoon jaunt. Near Central Park West and 77th Street I paused to gaze at ducks swimming across the iridescent watery expanse. During my reverie I heard a female voice: "Excuse me. Would you take my picture?" I turned to a smiling, young Asian woman holding out a camera.

"Sure," I replied.

The dappled Lake silhouetted her petite, curvy figure as I snapped a few shots. She appeared around twenty years old, five feet tall, wearing thick eyeglasses.

I handed her camera back, then she asked the classic question, "Do you live around here?"

I told her yes. A conversation ensued. Her English was fairly poor, but we managed to communicate. She was a Korean immigrant actually 28 years old, employed in a nail salon while studying English at Brooklyn College. In response to one of her questions I admitted that I was a writer. "Oh – I love writers!" she said.

We dined at Ollie's, a Chinese restaurant near Lincoln Center. She explained that she'd grown up in the vicinity of Seoul, beside a U.S. Army camp. The soldiers had been great guys, giving her and other kids candy and toys. "I love Americans," she announced happily. She also said that she wanted to start some kind of business and make lots of money.

When she smiled, I felt myself falling in love again. Evidently, I still carried romantic fantasy networks within my brain cells, although lacking certain necessary components in my physique.

As we departed the restaurant, she said, "I have always wanted to see a writer's apartment. Could I see yours?"

How could I deny a curious young mind opportunities to accumulate knowledge? "Sure."

We proceeded to my Hell's Kitchen residence, where disorder seemed not to faze her unduly. I turned on my high end stereo and selected the Chopin Nocturnes by Daniel Barenboim. We relaxed side by side on the sofa, not touching, eyes closed, spacing off. If I'd been normal, I'd ease into Don Juan routines. Instead, we listened to more Chopin. It was getting late. She said, "I do not feel like going home all the way to Brooklyn at night. Could I sleep here on the sofa?"

Far be it from me it to banish young ladies to dimly-lit, subway platforms, perhaps to be beaten and robbed. "Sure."

We showered (not at the same time) and went to bed around 11pm. I lay on my loft bed, she on the sofa. Mental pornographic movies starring the Asian nymph prevented sleep. If I were a real man, I'd be on her like a lion on a gazelle. But I'd become an emasculated alley cat experiencing needle-like sensations in my lower abdomen.

Dozing, around midnight, I heard footsteps on the ladder leading to my loft bed. "I want to be with you," she said.

She wore only a camisole and bikini underpants and

dropped into my arms. My head nearly exploded with surprise, joy, ecstasy of skin surfaces, etc. As half-baked intellectual, I couldn't help remembering Lolita and Humbert. He feared to make the first move on a teeny bopper so she seduced him. And something similar was happening to me, life imitating art yet again.

Regrettably there was one major obstacle to progress: no more erections. Instead, pressure increased inside my pelvis, along with occasional pinches of irritation. Although my senses were intoxicated by her fresh, young female warmth, I felt no eroticism whatever. The overall effect of this double whammy was extreme weirdness, but in the words of the immortal Hunter S. Thompson: "When the going gets weird, the weird turn pro."

I kissed her passionately, enacting all the usual motions like a puppet, while praying for a miracle. Unfortunately, no miracle arrived. She realized something was amiss. I explained my malady and she seemed genuinely touched, even seeking to comfort me. Activities then transpired during which I was tormented by near-total madness, augmented by dots of groinal pain. For the first time I comprehended true implications of that old dichotomy: the agony and the ecstasy.

Worst of all, my terrible secret was out. She knew I wasn't 100% man. Then I experienced the oddest and yukkiest orgasm of my life in some corner of my innards, accompanied by no ejaculation. I realized in that blazing instant that I never wanted to experience such fabulous but ultimately hellish sensations ever again.

Around 2am we lay side by side, staring at the ceiling, exchanging verbal intimacies. Out of the blue she asked, "Why don't we get married?"

I was speechless for several seconds, then replied,

"We've only known each other around twelve hours. We'll need to spend more time together and see if we're truly compatible."

In the darkness she slumbered at my side as I lay awake, pondering her suggestion. The most likely scenario was that she saw not a handsome, irresistible, silver cavalier in Central Park, sort of like Sean Connery, but instead she saw American citizenship as wife of a harmless-appearing geezer with midtown apartment, who radiated the aura of an ex-libertine. She only wanted to live the American dream and how could I fault her? I'd probably do the same if I was in her sneakers. And if I were a normal man – I would've married her on the spot.

Again, prostate cancer appeared a blessing in disguise. Because if we married, doubtlessly she'd desire a young man after a few months, cheat on me, break my heart, receive my rent-stabilized apartment and high-end stereo system in the divorce settlement, and totally ruin my life.

We saw each other twice more, never alone in my apartment. Her English remained fairly primitive despite college courses, so we couldn't have real conversations. I was working on a novel, and she was busy with school and the nail salon. Our "relationship" faded away.

A few months later, I spotted her sitting on a bench in Central Park, talking with a huge forty-something man with shaved head; he'd probably make three of her. She and I glanced at each other but didn't speak. Between us passed the clear understanding that she shouldn't be disturbed. Regarding her companion, Brad Pitt he wasn't but neither was I. He seemed completely absorbed by her unquestionable charm, as I'd been. He probably married her about a month later and presently she's an American citizen on her way to her first million dollars.

Following that unexpected sighting I descended to my usual eunuch groove, which meant accepting my fate stoically. Just when I thought my Erection Deficit Disorder was manageable, routine blood tests disclosed the return of prostate cancer. My New York City urologist explained that microscopic cancer cells evidently had been released into my bloodstream during surgery. Those cells were multiplying rapidly, soon to metastasize to bones, whereupon I'd undergo radiation and probably kick the bucket within the next "several years" or possibly within "a few years". But at least I needn't worry about Erection Deficit Disorder anymore.

I discussed my new cancerous condition on the phone with my daughter Debbie. We agreed that I should pass my final years in the bosom of my family. So I gave up my rent-stabilized apartment in midtown Manhattan and moved in with Debbie and her husband Dan in Aurora, Illinois. Surrounded by love, I psyched myself for the inevitable passage to Hades.

But after arriving in Illinois, each time my blood was tested, less cancer was identified. Inexplicably, miracle of miracles, my cancer was going into remission. It looked like I'd live after all, glorious news except for three major drawbacks: (1) I was far from my home base, New York City, (2) I couldn't afford to return, and (3) no more erections.

I decided that I needed my own apartment, so moved to a small, low rent farm town (pop. 3,100) in northwestern Illinois, around 120 miles west of Chicago, surrounded by corn and soybean fields, hog barns and cattle grazing, far off the beaten track.

But I still must go to the supermarket. And I've

learned that country women in faded blue jeans and T-shirts are as lovely as mid-Manhattan ladies wearing latest Prada, Gucci and Armani fashions.

Apparently beautiful women are everywhere, even in obscure corners of the planet such as the Rock River Valley of Illinois. Clearly I cannot escape them no matter where I relocate. "My doom is sealed," as they say in Victorian novels.

To adjust, I've tried to be rational. As honest people will admit, romance is not always as terrific as advertised. Sometimes people aren't attuned to each other for whatever reason. Or one partner falls deeply in love while the second is merely screwing around. Sometimes people tire of lovers whom they'd previously promised to adore till the end of time. Familiarity breeds contempt, they say. Occasionally lovers murder their beloveds out of jealousy. So the mating game isn't always a party and no sane person should remove her/his clothes and dive into bed on a whim.

Despite my rationalizations, moralizations and self-deceptions, women continue to bedazzle me. I cannot live without them, but I must. We human beings evidently cannot escape breeding programming regardless of our determination to do so, even when we lose erotic feelings and abilities due to prostate cancer surgery. How can I ignore women shoppers in the mall or at the supermarket? The answer is: I can't.

Obviously I need to: (1) Accept reality and stop kvetching already; (2) Be grateful for abilities I still have; and (3) Enjoy life to the extent I still can.

After all, I still have the love of my children and grandchildren. I also have wonderful friends, books to read, music, movies, the joys of travel, delicious Chinese, Mexican and Italian restaurants, and my unending passion for writing novels that not many people want to read.

And I still can enjoy the company of lovely women who truly are much more than sexual gratification machines, who can be fascinating intellectually and spiritually, and often provide useful professional and personal advice.

In a larger sense, my misfortune seems relatively minor compared to soldiers whose legs were blown off by roadside bombs, or people who go blind, or are paralyzed by strokes and confined to wheelchairs, or are stricken with Alzheimer's disease and can't even recognize their children. No one can expect to go through life trouble free, and thankfully I still can walk, have all my visible body parts plus most of my marbles, and should be grateful that I got off so easy.

Besides, nothing bad ever happens to a writer. It's all material.

48

HARD-BOILED CRIME

AFTER SETTLING DOWN IN THIS SMALL ILLINOIS TOWN (current population 3000), the first standalone novel that I worked on was *Web Of Doom*, a hard-boiled crime melodrama set in New York City during the 1990s, about a tough ex-NYPD cop accused of the brutal murder of a beautiful socialite in a Times Square hotel.

He'd never even met the victim, but circumstantial evidence points directly to him. He must solve the crime or do the time. Lethal injection is not out of the question, therefore he is highly motivated to identify the perp, and not averse to busting heads of those impeding his investigation.

This novel was the result of many elements bouncing around in my head during the 1990s.

One element was inserted into my skull on April 17, 1994 when I was sitting alone in my funky apartment in Hell's Kitchen, Manhattan, reading the New York Times. I came across the following headline:

BRATTON SAYS CORRUPTION SWEEP

INVOLVES DOZEN MORE OFFICERS
Cites Widespread Collusion in Bronx Precinct

This story about corrupt cops really caught my attention. I'd been living in the Big Apple since 1961 and it seemed that every few years a major police corruption scandal erupted. I was intrigued by these cops who swore to uphold the law but became corrupt due to temptation for money, because temptation for money is hard to beat.

Around that time I was hanging out occasionally with a guy named Jack Baxter who was around 15 or 20 years younger than I, son of a former press agent colleague of mine, the legendary Billy Baxter who became a film distributor and now has passed away.

Jack was around 6 feet 4 inches tall, built like an athlete, curly dark blond hair, baby face. He wrote for the *New York Post* and was producing documentary films.

Jack grew up in a Bronx street-fighting neighborhood and still was in touch with many of his old male and female friends. They often partied together, and Jack invited me to accompany him to some of these blowouts. While speaking with Jack and the others, I became interested in Bronx culture which seemed more down to earth and real than Manhattan snobbery and pretentiousness, but evidently had been quite violent. Young men showed their valor by going outside and getting into fights, like the Jets and Sharks in *West Side Story*.

Jack liked bars and introduced me to Kennedy's on West 57th Street between 8th and 9th Avenues. Kennedy's was a classy joint frequented by many off-duty NYPD police officers, detectives, FBI agents and other law enforcement, including their ladies or random single women who dropped in.

Kennedy's was located around two blocks east of a big CBS studio building, and also attracted many CBS executives, administrative types, technicians like cameramen, and producer types.

The cops that I met at Kennedy's were not simple-minded flatfoots. Most had college credits and were intelligent and ambitious. They dressed nicely, not like slobs. The women were upscale and also well dressed. I thought Kennedy's one of the most interesting bars that I ever visited during my 42 years in New York City.

Jack realized that I was curious about cop culture so decided to take me to a cop community in the Far Rock-away neighborhood of Queens. We rode out on a subway line that had been the scene of a murder the day before. I was a little nervous, but Jack was a big rough guy and I hoped we could handle any threat as long as no guns or knives were involved.

Finally, we came to this bucolic community of cottages between Long Island sound and a boardwalk. The first building we saw was a bar, naturally. We walked past it and came to a bunch of people talking in the middle of a street on which there was no vehicular traffic. Jack knew many of the people, introduced me around, and one of the guys I met was a notorious former cop named Tommy Ryan better known as Nutsy Ryan.

Jack previously had told me about Nutsy who was renowned throughout the NYPD because he had gone to prison for a murder he claimed not to have committed. A certain notorious drug dealer had been beaten to death while in police custody. Nutsy took the fall for a 51-month sentence in which he was fighting for his life regularly against incarcerated criminals who hated cops.

Nutsy looked like a mean, dangerous guy. He had

straight black hair about two inches long standing at a slant atop his head, suspicious eyes, straight nose, grim mouth and chin like the prow of a ship. He basically ignored me probably because I wasn't a cop, therefore unworthy of respect. I was very impressed by his menacing physical presence and story, and never forgot him.

Also around that time I read a true crime book called *Buddy Boys* by Mike McAlary about corruption in Brooklyn's 77th Precinct known as "the Alamo" in the crime-ridden Bedford-Stuyvesant and Crown Heights neighborhoods during the 1970's. This is a great book and educated me further about the prevalence of NYC police corruption.

In the mid-90s when finally I sat down to write my hard-boiled crime melodrama, all the above elements came together in my mind. I wanted to create a noirish crime story that would launch a series like Sam Spade, Philip Marlowe, Mike Hammer, etc. I had high hopes for this novel and thought of it as my future meal ticket and retirement income.

As stated previously, all my novels begin with a main character. I decided that for this one the main character would be Patrick Shapiro, an Irish-Jewish cop based partially on Nutsy Ryan and me, which made him a rugged character like Nutsy plus half-baked intellectual nut job like me.

Patty is a disgraced ex-cop from the corrupt precinct in the Bronx mentioned in the *Times* article above. He was not corrupt himself but looked the other way and never ratted out buddy boys who engaged in various criminal activities such as selling confiscated cocaine, taking bribes, beating up criminals, and on slow nights, committing robberies in uniform. He got tossed by the

NYPD for not reporting crimes committed in his presence.

He lives in my dingy apartment in Hell's Kitchen, where else? When the novel opens, he's in his pad, recently fired from the NYPD, nearly broke, on the verge of becoming homeless, seriously contemplating suicide. The phone rings. The caller is one of his former buddy boys who has heard about a dirty job, to photograph a cheating wife in bed with her boyfriend in a midtown hotel for her jealous angry husband's divorce case.

A few days later, Patty gains entry to the hotel room at 2am, and finds the lady alone, her throat slashed, dead. He calls 911. Homicide detectives arrive and think Patty did the deed because they consider him a crooked cop capable of any violation including bloody murder. Patty must solve the crime or do the time.

I thought this situation an excellent propellant for the narrative. Patty's investigation takes him all over Manhattan, from Hell's Kitchen to the Broadway area, fashionable East Side, Chelsea, Little Italy, Chinatown, Soho, the East Village, even Fire Island. A few more related murders occur, Patty gets thrown into jail for a while, and eventually solves the crime although getting shot (not quite fatally) in the process.

I thought I achieved all my goals with this novel and was very proud of it, but my literary agent was unable to make a sale. Not every writer sells every one of his novels. Not every writer becomes a star. Some writers strike out.

Many years later, I mentioned *Web Of Doom* on Facebook, which prompted James Reasoner of Rough Edges Press to contact me and offer to publish it.

James gave it an excellent eye-catching cover

designed by his wife Livia. *Web Of Doom* now is available in paper and ebooks. I wrote the following lines for jacket copy, which sums up the novel's essence:

> *What is evidence? Who is innocent?*
> *Can justice really prevail in a city*
> *where the law is just another commodity*
> *betrayal is business as usual*
> *and paranoia is mental health?*

49

MY GREAT AMERICAN CIVIL WAR NOVEL

I NEVER THOUGHT OF WRITING A CIVIL WAR NOVEL UNTIL one afternoon approximately 1995 when I was sitting in the office of my then literary agent Nancy Yost in an office building just east of Pennsylvania Station in New York City.

I was wondering out loud what to write next when Nancy suggested a mystery novel set in New York City during the Civil War, in the manner of Ann Perry. I'm no Ann Perry but it sounded like a great idea. I said I'd do it.

A tremendous amount of research was required. I joined the New-York Historical Society to use their specialized library in their beautiful Beaux Arts-style palace on Central Park West at 77th Street.

Every day for around a month I walked uptown to the Society, arrived at opening time, read books like a college student preparing for an exam, lunched in the neighborhood, returned to the Society, departed at closing time, and walked back to my apartment on West 55th Street on the eastern edge of the neighborhood known as Hell's Kitchen.

Finally my head was bursting with info about New York City during the Civil War. The time had come to sit and write. My goal was a great towering Civil War novel that would blow away Margaret Mitchell's *Gone with the Wind*, Michael Shaara's *Killer Angels*, and Stephen Crane's *The Red Badge of Courage*.

I conceived the basic plot as a murder mystery with lots of interesting ramifications. Someone is murdering prominent Wall Street financiers in 1861, a few months after the Battle of Bull Run, first major battle of the Civil War.

Is the culprit one or more disgruntled investors? Insane Marxist revolutionaries? A Confederate conspiracy to destabilize the Union banking system? The investor's disaffected son? The investor's wife whom many considered a selfish horrible bitch? Or someone else not so obvious? Or a combination of the above?

To complicate matters further, a massive crime wave engulfed New York City following the outbreak of the Civil War, as if that tumultuous conflict loosened the darkest passions in the hearts of men and women. Robberies, burglaries and assaults became commonplace, including garrotings on Fifth Avenue in broad daylight!!!

The Detective Precinct is under political pressure to arrest whoever is killing financiers, but the best detectives have enlisted in New York regiments.

Out of desperation, Deputy Chief of Detectives Timothy Flanagan hires a limping former Union army officer wounded recently in the Battle of Bull Run, and a former Southern Belle stranded in the great Empire City. Flanagan calls her his secretary because women can't be detectives, but she carries a revolver and does actual detective work.

The ex-officer is a staunch outspoken abolitionist, while the ex-Southern Belle passionately hates abolitionists, blaming them for the invasion of Dixie. Naturally they loathe each other on their deepest levels but must work together to solve the crime. Their frequent arguments explore, in a manner that I considered brilliant, all issues that led to the Civil War.

Their investigations take them from Fifth Avenue mansions to the dangerous slum called Five Points, from Gramercy Park to Battery Park, from fashionable men's clubs to elegant and not so elegant brothels, gambling dens, the glittering Broadway theater district, colorful Bowery, and the Peyster Street docks where a man's life isn't worth a dead mackerel.

Along the way the reader will encounter actual historical figures such as banker J.P. Morgan, newspaperman Horace Greeley, Chief of the Union Intelligence Service Allan Pinkerton, Confederate Senator Robert Barnwell Rhett, real estate tycoon William Backhouse Astor, Archbishop John Hughes of the New York City Archdiocese, young Billy the Kid, artist John Frederick Kensett, poet Walt Whitman, recent West Point grad Lieutenant George Armstrong Custer, an actor named John Wilkes Booth, members of a criminal gang known as the Dead Rabbits, and the controversial mayor of New York City, Fernando Wood.

During the investigation, the ex-officer often is disturbed by flashbacks of Bull Run, its massive artillery barrages, thousands of bullets whistling through the air, and Confederate soldiers trying to stab their bayonets into him. The Union Army had been pushed back and he nearly got killed, experiences that still haunt him. I read two history books devoted to Bull Run and numerous references in other Civil War histories to make sure I got details right.

Will the Detective Precinct solve the case? They dare not fail. The future of the war and fate of the nation is at stake!

Finally I finished the novel and felt absolutely certain it proved conclusively that I was a great American novelist ranking with the best of all time. Finally I would receive the critical adulation I so richly deserved, not to mention hundreds of thousands if not millions of dollars in royalties, and a major Hollywood movie deal.

I proudly delivered the novel to Nancy who promptly submitted it to publishers. An editor at Bantam wanted to publish it and said he was "a fan" of min, but was over-ruled by other editors. Every other publisher contacted by Nancy rejected my great American Civil War novel.

To say that I was disappointed would be too mild. I couldn't believe that this novel could be rejected every-where when novels that I considered far inferior were being published and earning huge amounts for their authors. Gradually I came to the awful realization that my entire so-called literary career probably was a terrible mistake, horrible joke, utter catastrophe, and in reality I was nothing more than a deluded fool.

I re-thought and re-edited *Grip Of Death* for several years, improving it considerably. Finally around 2018 I thought it time for another shot at publication, but had nowhere to submit it because I found it very difficult to make contact with former editors, as if they had iron walls around them to protect them from the likes of me.

Meanwhile, Nancy had become a big-time agent with her own staff and office. After jumping through many hoops, I finally made phone contact with her and became deeply hurt when she said she wasn't interested in reading my wonderful newly re-written version of *Grip Of Death*, never mind representing it, although it had been *her idea* in the first place. Evidently, obviously, she didn't think much of my writing abilities which broke my heart yet again and sent me into a funk which probably never will go away completely.

A few years later, I mentioned *Grip Of Death* on Facebook. James Reasoner of Rough Edges Press offered to publish it. He gave it an excellent cover designed by his wife Livia, and now finally *Grip Of Death* is available as paperbacks and ebooks.

It is selling very poorly, I'm sorry to say. Am I just another crazy self-deceived author? Or a shamefully neglected, extraordinarily talented author? What in the hell happened to me? In the immortal words of my dear old departed friend Gloria Wilcher: "Go know."

50

MY ALL-TIME FAVORITE NOVEL

COBRA WOMAN IS MY ALL-TIME FAVORITE NOVEL OF THE 86 that I wrote and were published. It also is the first novel I ever completed and last to be published.

I love all my novels but love this one most. It is far more ambitious than anything I'd ever written. One could even call it my magnum opus, the pinnacle of my so-called literary career. I worked very hard to make it a smoothly flowing entertainment for intelligent people.

Not a murder mystery, war novel, Western saga, spy melodrama or other type of genre novel, it is about a horrible, funny marriage, based on my first marriage.

Cobra Woman began under another title and concept in 1965 when I was a 30-year-old press agent for 20th Century-Fox and drowning in a catastrophic marriage because my dear wife and I proved to be incompatible on our deepest levels after only a few months together.

The marriage seemed so utterly bizarre and ridiculous – I felt compelled to write about it, perhaps because I wanted to better understand how I got into such a complicated mess, and also because I had wanted to write a novel for around ten years but never could determine a theme. At last I had found a theme, my totally insane marriage.

I married a Cuban refugee named Nirania who had been a showgirl/dancer in the famed Tropicana in Old Havana before Castro. It was said that the most beautiful women in Cuba were showgirls and dancers at the Tropicana.

When I met her she was married, separated from her husband and vacationing in New York City, but her home was in the Miami suburb of Hialeah. The romantic setting of Nirania's and my first great encounter was a party in the West 80s near Central Park. I had been invited by my friend Mike Nichols whom I've mentioned many times before.

I looked across the crowded room and there she was. Our eyes met and my life veered off in an entirely new direction.

I hit on her, somehow we fell in love, she got divorced, we married, she got pregnant, and we had a baby girl, Deborah. She had two daughters aged three and six from her first marriage, and they became my wonderful stepdaughters, Francesca and Diana. Their father was said to be in the Mafia.

Nirania was very jealous and could get violent quickly. As a dancer she was quite strong, and her punches had steam on them. Yet she also had a delightful sense of humor, often was fun to be around, was a great dancer, and had a lovely singing voice. In other words, she was a complicated, interesting person who murdered the English language whenever she opened her mouth. She would say "washbrained" instead of "brainwashed" and often commented, "I have only been in this country a short distance." When angry at me she called me a "mizzable sneaky traitor".

Prior to getting married, while living in Greenwich Village, I began numerous novels but mainly imitated Jack Kerouac and never got very far into completing any of them probably because I was not Kerouac and didn't think like him. My problem was that I didn't have anything to write about. Mere desire to write a novel was not enough.

While married to Nirania, as mentioned above, I finally had something to write about: my crazy marriage. The novel is also about direct-mail advertising, which drew on my actual experiences as a copywriter for Prentice-Hall circa 1961. It also is about human nuttiness in New York City and Miami at the dawn of the Internet Age.

I completed the first version in 1971. My then literary agent Elaine Markson thought it wonderful. "I'm gonna sell this," she told me confidently. She submitted it to several major publishers and received several rejections.

I was disappointed or perhaps "crushed" would be more accurate because I expected publication right off the bat, earning tons of money from the advance and royalties, getting optioned by Hollywood, vaulting me to the very forefront of American literature, possibly even winning the National Book Award, with the Nobel Prize not out of the question. I could even see myself on the Johnny Carson Show, telling witty stories about my life, loves and numerous crackpot misadventures.

What went wrong other than my own absurd expectations? I'm not the kind of novelist who cries about publishers and editors not appreciating my allegedly great genius. Instead, I rethought and rewrote the novel

LEN LEVINSON

several times as years passed. Elaine and other literary agents submitted various versions to publishers. It was rejected again and again but I was unable to give it up because, somehow, I still believed in the story.

In the 1980s I updated the narrative to escape its Vietnam War era baggage that I felt detracted from essential plot lines. I also re-imagined fundamental plot elements from a more mature perspective as I myself matured. I kept rewriting and rethinking *Cobra Woman*, trying to create a perfect work of literary art although there are no perfect works of art, but I considered the effort necessary and even noble because the pursuit of literary excellence is noble.

And the plot is personal, inspired by the first great love of my life, which I considered a unique maladroit extravaganza, or perhaps "fiasco" would be a better description of that powerful life-shattering experience that brought me to the center of myself and showed me who I really am: a screwball of cosmic proportions.

One can view life as comedy or tragedy. I prefer comedy but tragedy cannot completely be excluded from real-life relations between men and women, because love not always is a many-splendored thing.

I worked on this novel for over a half-century, sometimes on and off, other times intensively for long periods of time. A few years ago, I reached a point where I could find nothing more to rewrite or rethink. Finally, it was complete. I submitted it to a literary agent who previously had sold numerous of my novels to the majors. She rejected it with one sentence: "I don't think I can sell it."

She didn't elaborate on why she didn't think she could sell it, which left me guessing. I knew that getting published by a major publisher is extremely difficult these days, especially if the author previously wrote 83 published novels and never had a hit.

Only an Indie publisher would dare take it on. That's James Reasoner at Rough Edges Press, who already had published two of my novels. He is a man of courage and extraordinary literary taste, not to mention a gentleman, scholar and author of nearly 400 published novels himself!!!

Indie publishers don't have the same marketing clout as the majors. My great magnum opus has been selling extremely poorly.

Amazingly, I have no regrets. Writing *Cobra Woman* was worth the effort regardless of financial considerations. It was a great literary adventure, a mind-blowing journey of self-discovery, and a helluva rollercoaster ride. I'm very pleased with results of my long labor, except it wasn't labor but a pleasurable challenge most of the time.

Many readers have told me, in person or on the internet, that they enjoyed *Cobra Woman* and it would make a great movie.

My granddaughter, Rachel, age 17, wrote an unsolicited review of Cobra Woman. Among her comments were:

It took me under 24 hours to read this novel, as it was quite captivating and held my attention the whole way through.

The reader immediately finds themselves swept into the life of a New Yorker living in a city that is truly alive. The reader can see the world clearly through the narrator's eyes, and the whirlwind romance that ensues is both hilarious and tragic.

The book is infused with humor and deals with the human experience in a relatable way. The reader is able to

*touch the frustration, love, thoughts, happiness, and sadness
that the narrator experiences.*

*Thank you, grandpa, for writing this book. I absolutely
loved it and was laughing a lot watching Sam navigate the
situations he found himself in. I thought you did a fantastic
job creating the setting and developing the characters to be
larger than life. Every character played an integral role. I
look forward to reading more of your novels in the future!"*

Rachel is a tough, discerning reader. She doesn't like
everything she reads. *Cobra Woman* cannot possibly be a
dud if she and many others appreciated it.

Cobra Woman by Len Levinson now is available as a
trade paperback and ebook, if anyone's interested.

51

MY WONDERFUL STONED
HEART ATTACK

IN 2012, DURING THE TIME I WHILE WORKING ON THE three previously mentioned novels:

Web Of Doom

Grip Of Death

Cobra Woman

I had a full-blown heart attack. Here's how it went down:

Throughout most of my life, one of my worst fears was having a medical emergency while under the influence of marijuana. I thought the horrors of the medical crisis would be magnified exponentially by marijuana and freak me out of my head. But like the devout viper I was, I couldn't allow this fear to stop me from smoking.

So it came to pass that I actually had a medical emergency while under the influence of marijuana. It occurred Sunday morning 4/22/2012 when I was 76 years old, lying on my sofa here in rural northwest Illinois, gazing out the big picture window at the sky, experiencing profound mystical thoughts—or so I thought at the time—when I became aware of what seemed to be increasing stomach gas pains intruding themselves into my reveries, dragging me back to reality. So I chewed two GAS-X pills. They didn't help. I chewed two more. No relief. Then I drank Mylanta. Nothing. Meanwhile I was zonked out of my skull, with my so-called mind vaulting into higher celestial realms, as the pain became worse.

I finally decided that Alka-Seltzer surely would do the trick but didn't have any in my pad. I couldn't drive or walk to the store because of intense pain in my upper stomach and/or lower chest, so I managed to stagger stoned next door to the fire department and ask for Alka-Seltzer. Nick, the emergency medical person on duty, said they had no Alka-Seltzer, suggested I was having a heart attack, and asked if he could do an EKG. I said okay, followed him to the ambulance where the EKG was located, and laid down, my head still spinning with cannabis space-outs.

Nick peered at squiggly lines on the monitor and said something like: "It looks like you're having a heart attack." He asked me to take a nitroglycerine pill. I refused because I believed I only was experiencing unusually terrible stomach gas pains, which were influencing the EKG.

In retrospect, I probably feared open heart surgery wherein doctors buzzsaw open the breastbone and pull back ribs. The mere thought, intensified by weed induced fantasies, produced sheer overwhelming terror in my mind.

Nick recommended that I go to the nearest emergency room and get checked out. "Your heart is acting real funny." I retorted that my heart was acting funny because of gas pains, a statement totally ridiculous biologically, but spoken with my usual drugged-crazed self-assurance, as if I really knew what I was talking about.

Finally, I gave in because I couldn't handle the pain anymore. Another emergency medical person named Breanna drove the ambulance over country roads lined with recently-planted corn and soybean fields. During the trip, Nick implored me to take at least one nitroglycerine pill; finally, I relented.

The nearest emergency room was in Dixon, where Ronald Reagan grew up, about 25 miles away. Nick called ahead and discovered they had no cardiac team on duty that Sunday. So Breanna drove to the Community General Hospital (CGH) in Sterling, around 35 miles away. My pain was so intense, I was writhing, squirming and gasping, unable to get comfortable, while my cannabis saturated brain cells kept tripping into the stratosphere. During the ambulance ride I had an out of body experience as if I was looking down at myself contorted and twisted with increasingly severe pain.

When finally, I arrived at the emergency room, the cardiac team was waiting. An EKG was done immediately, followed by some kind of imaging test, after which Doctor Paul Maxwell said I was having a heart attack and needed to go to the cardiac lab right away. Again, I argued that I only was having a gas attack that was mimicking a heart attack, although I had no idea what I was talking about, as often is the case.

Doctor Maxwell got in my face and announced, to the best of my recollection: "Mr. Levinson – you're having a massive heart attack. If we don't act quickly, you're going to die."

Finally, I surrendered unconditionally. Young women

nurses tore off my clothes, which would have been delightful under other circumstances. Another advanced with a battery-powered device that shaved hair from my groin, in preparation for the catheter insertion which would explore my heart. Intravenous lines were installed into my arms. I signed a document stating that I didn't want my daughter Debbie notified yet, because I feared she'd also have a heart attack. Then they shot me up with Demerol, which made me feel wonderful, paradoxically despite pain, and finally I was wheeled to the cardiac lab, where nurses worked busily around me for a minute or two, and then...

I opened my eyes in the Critical Care Unit, hooked up to all manner of intravenous and other beeping machines, a blood pressure cuff on my left arm, oxygen tubes up my nose. My chest pain was gone; no longer was I stoned. After a while, Dr. Maxwell arrived and reported that one artery had been 100% blocked, a second 70% blocked and a third 30% blocked. He had installed stents in the first two and would stent the third in a couple of weeks when I was stronger. I didn't need open heart surgery because the catheter was able to break through the plaque, which is impacted cholesterol.

Although drugged and debilitated, I asked: "How could this happen to me? I hike for around two hours, six days a week. I also do calisthenics and work out with weights for around 45 minutes on six mornings per week."

He replied: "If it weren't for that exercise, the heart attack would've killed you." Then he explained that my clogging heart developed "collateral pathways" during exercise, which ultimately saved me.

I protested: "But I'm around 90% vegetarian. How could I have all that cholesterol?"

He replied: "You could eat nothing but grass all your life, and still develop this condition because our livers produce cholesterol at genetically determined rates." He added that my heart was damaged, but heart muscle can rejuvenate. In about a year I'd probably be healthier than before the heart attack.

I slept most of the day in a coma-like condition. The next day, I called Debbie, who did not flip out as I expected. She said she'd leave ASAP for the hospital. Meanwhile, I was feeling considerably better, and Doctor Maxwell suggested I try to walk. I interpreted this to mean a license to hike around the hospital, which led to deep exhaustion and collapse into bed. Later, a nurse told me that heart attack victims often refuse to admit they're having or have had heart attacks. Another nurse said that when people get older, they should expect medical problems.

Debbie drove approximately 100 miles from her home in Aurora to the hospital. She told me later that she cried all the way, but upon arrival became ice cold logical, asking pertinent questions and taking notes.

25 April, Wednesday: I was wheeled, accompanied by Debbie, to the nuclear medicine clinic for a nuclear scan. Next day Dr. Maxwell said the scan was "fantastic".

27 April, Friday: I was released from CGH feeling quite chipper. Debbie drove me home. That night I woke up wrathful, cursing, gnashing my teeth, punching my pillow, furious that I couldn't resume my normal life, not wanting to take so many powerful, scary medications with all sorts of side effects that slowed me down. My shenanigans woke up Debbie, who calmly explained that I needed to adapt to the reality of my heart attack and getting angry at my own heart wouldn't aid my recovery. I couldn't refute her ironclad logic, so went back to bed

and slept deeply. She stayed with me until 29 April Sunday, when she needed to go home and take care of her family.

30 April, Monday: Chest pains returned in earnest. I thought I was having another heart attack, but this time wasn't stoned. Again, I hobbled to the fire station. A medical technician named Joy was on duty. She did an EKG and said results were unclear, perhaps because I'd recently had a heart attack. She suggested I go to the emergency room and get checked out. I refused at first but finally gave in again because of searing pain. A female technician named Bobbie drove the ambulance to CGH, as I tried to sing that old Nat King Cole song: "I just found Joy" to Joy, who stared at me in disbelief.

In the CGH emergency room, they ran an EKG and other tests, determining I wasn't having another heart attack. Instead, they diagnosed Dressler's Syndrome, an inflammation of the sac surrounding the heart, a disorder that affects about 7% of people who have heart attacks.

Medical personnel treated the inflammation with large doses of ibuprofen which caused kidney failure, water in the lungs and fainting. I ended up back in the Critical Care Unit, hooked to intravenous drips intended to flush ibuprofen from my system, and with oxygen tubes up my nose. Then they administered colchicine, another anti-inflammatory med ordinarily given to gout patients.

Debbie returned to the hospital, which made me very happy. She visited all day every day I was there, and during nights slept in my pad.

May 4, Friday: Two more stents were installed via catheter around 6pm. Dr. Maxwell was on vacation, so Dr. Thomas Kurian performed the procedure. He reported afterwards that he ran a stress test on my heart which indicated good functioning. Sometime later, a nurse told me that I'd need seven days of recuperation for every day in the hospital, which ultimately would amount to 90-odd days of recuperation.

6 May, Sunday: I was released from the hospital, Debbie drove me home, and that evening I nearly fainted in the shower. If Debbie wasn't there, I might've cracked my skull on the tiles. Later my neighbors in this HUD senior citizen residence, most of whom have had heart attacks, strokes, diabetic seizures, etc., advised me not to take showers with the door closed, because steam and decreased oxygen would knock me out.

RNs visited every other day to monitor progress or regress. Debbie stayed till Friday 11 May, when she returned home after a total of three weeks with me. I don't think I could've survived without her. Her loving care and analytical thinking were critical to my sense of wellbeing. Our time together provided many opportunities for conversations during which we ironed out certain misunderstandings and confusions that had developed over the years. As I look back on my life, I think it's accurate to say that I've loved her more than anyone else I've ever known. She'll always be my baby girl, although she then was 46.

After Debbie left, I still felt weak and afflicted with mild to moderate random chest pain which I assumed was Dressler's Syndrome but felt like mini-heart attacks and quite troubling. On 17 May, Thursday, I returned to CGH for a scheduled appointment with Dr. Maxwell, got an EKG, and told him about weakness and pain. He and his nurse practitioner Polly examined me and scheduled an angiogram for 22 May, Tuesday, which meant another catheter into my groin, to discover if my heart valves were leaking, and/or whether I needed more stents, and/or open heart surgery.

After the angiogram date was set, I returned home and felt increasingly weak with lots of chest pain. On 22 May, Tuesday, Debbie drove me to CGH for the angiogram. During prep, one nurse told me that having a heart attack is "like getting hit by a Mack truck", and I might need to accept weakness and fatigue as "your new normal". But other nurses said I might get stronger. Then I was wheeled into the cardiac lab and soon became unconscious.

Sometime later (approximately 45 minutes according to Debbie), I woke up on the operating table and was wheeled back to the Critical Care Unit. Dr. Maxwell arrived shortly thereafter and said my heart was stronger than recorded at my last angiogram, my arteries were clear, no valve leakage, but a small section of my heart remained damaged, and I'd developed atrial fibrillation aka arrythmia, which nurses call "A-fib". New meds were prescribed to combat chest pain and A-fib.

On 23 May, Wednesday, I returned home and was taking nine meds, which caused dizziness, weakness and disorientation. I spent much time flat on my back in a coma-like state. I read books and magazines when I was strong enough to think, and if I felt really powerful, worked on this essay in an attempt to understand what happened to me.

After around a month of recuperation, I reported three times per week for cardiac rehab which lasted six weeks. The nurses told me that "exercise strengthens the heart". Cardiac rehab was like a health club where patients exercised on machines while hooked up to ekg monitors. The big benefit was that I could exercise strenuously without fear of a heart attack because registered nurses were there. Gradually I was weaned off most of my meds. Gradually my A-fib went away. Gradually my full strength returned. One year after my heart attack, as Doctor Maxwell predicted, I felt better than before the heart attack.

I no longer smoke marijuana, drink booze or caffeine, and have become a vegetarian most of the time. It's kind of boring but I'd rather be alive.

How can heart attacks be predicted? Get a stress test, although some medical writers claim stress tests can produce false positives and negatives. But get one anyway to be on the safe side. And get a C-reactive protein test, which is a blood test that predicts heart disease. Doctors also recommend regular exercise and reduction of animal fats, salt, sugar and carbs that produce triglycerides. Avoid a heart attack if you can, because they're quite painful and can do serious damage, such as kill you.

Both my cardiologists believe an all-plant diet can prevent and reverse heart attacks. Some cardiologists and nutritionists believe that heart attacks are caused partly by deficiencies of Vitamins B6, B12 and folic acid.

My heart attack actually was a blessing in disguise, because it forced me to adopt a healthier lifestyle which probably will prolong my life. I now feel great, can do anything I want, such as hike for one and one-half to two hours virtually every day. If it weren't for modern medicine and drugs, I'd be crematorium smoke floating in the atmosphere. Now I can look forward to another ten or even twenty years on this planet, which itself seems to be in very poor health, falling apart before my very eyes.

52

LOOKING BACK AT MY LITERARY CAREER

AT AGE OF 85, AS I LOOK BACK AT MY LITERARY CAREER, uppermost in my mind is the realization that I really enjoyed writing each of my 86 published novels, although admittedly novel writing isn't always easy, and I never made much dough.

I'm not complaining. In fact, I'm very grateful that destiny or perhaps luck or whatever talent I possessed allowed me to be a freelance novelist from 1971 until now except for a few gaps here and there.

I wanted to be a writer since the fifth grade, as described previously. Becoming a professional novelist became my grandest dream that later actually came true. I was my own boss which meant I didn't need to deal with supervisors, office politics, pressure to work harder, and all other crap that working people need to tolerate. I truly enjoyed playing around in my imagination. At least I loved my job. At least I did it my way.

It's true that my books never sold well, and I subsisted on the ragged unstable edges of the economy for most of my tumultuous literary career. It's true that I ended up in a psycho ward for 28 hours. Many times, I wished I had become an accountant or librarian, fighter pilot, sailor in the U.S. Navy, electronics engineer, long distance truck driver, history professor, psychologist, oncologist, or some other career providing steady paychecks.

But when I think about it more comprehensively – I had no choice. Writing novels was a powerful compulsion, a deep-rooted need to express myself which I could not ignore.

Where did this deep-rooted need come from? Perhaps from being an only child who spent much time alone reading comic books during my early years. As mentioned before, my mother died when I was four and dear old Dad and I kept different hours; I seldom saw him.

That was the era before television. I listened to the radio or read comic books or gazed into the middle distance, spinning fantasies in my mind, usually about feats of derring-do starring me admired by girls with whom I went to school.

I usually had no one to talk with at home so communicated with myself silently through the medium of stories I told myself. If I had grown up with a mother, father and siblings with whom I spoke regularly, perhaps I never would have become a novelist.

According to Georges Simenon: "I think that anyone who does not 'need' to be a writer, who thinks he can do something else, ought to do something else. Writing is not a profession but a vocation of unhappiness."

Writing novels was not a vocation of unhappiness for me, although I had many setbacks and doubts. But otherwise, Simenon's statement rang true. It seemed that I could do nothing else. I hated every job I ever had because every job became repetitious and boring after the first few weeks or months.

Writing never was boring for me. It was the royal road to understanding myself and the world and provided me with pleasures and delights that sustained me during my roughest times.

Best of all, many people have said that they appreciated my books. That is the greatest reward of all.

ALSO BY LEN LEVINSON

The Apache Wars Saga series
by pseudonym Frank Burleson
originally published by Signet
available as e-books by Len Levinson

1. *Desert Hawks* 1994

2.. *War Eagles* 1995

3. *Savage Frontier* 1995

4. *White Apache* 1996

5. *Devil Dance* 1997

6. *Night of the Cougar* 1997

The Pecos Kid series
by Jack Bodine
published by Harper Paperbacks
available as e-books by Len Levinson

1. *Beginner's Luck* 1992

2. *The Reckoning* 1993

3. *Apache Moon* 1993

4. *Outlaw Hell* 1993

5. *Devil's Creek Massacre* 1994

6. *Bad to the Bone* 1994

The Rat Bastards series

by John Mackie

published by Jove Books

available as e-books by Len Levinson

1. *Hit The Beach* 1983

2. *Death Squad* 1983

3. *River Of Blood* 1983

4. *Meat Grinder Hill* 1984

5. *Down and Dirty* 1984

6. *Green Hell* 1984

7. *Too Mean to Die* 1984

8. *Hot Lead and Cold Steel* 1984

9. *Do or Die* 1984

10. *Kill Crazy* 1984

11. *Nightmare Alley* 1985

12. *Go For Broke* 1985

13. *Tough Guys Die Hard* 1985

14. *Suicide River* 1985

15. *Satan's Cage* 1985

16. *Go Down Fighting* 1985

The Sergeant series

by Gordon Davis

published by Zebra and Bantam

available as e-books by Len Levinson

1. *Death Train* 1980

The Skymasters series

by Richard Hale Curtis

published by Dell

Has been republished under my real name as an ebook and paperback.

Freedom Fighters series

by Jonathan Scofield

published by Dell

Has been republished under my real name as an ebook and paperback.

The Silent Service series

by J. Farragut Jones

published by Dell

Has been republished under my real name as ebooks and paperbacks.

2. *Forty Fathoms Down* 1981

5. *Tracking The Wolf Pack* 1981

Butler series

by Philip Kirk

published by Leisure Books

some available as e-books by Len Levinson

1. *The Hydra Conspiracy* 1979

2. *Smart Bombs* 1979

3. *The Slayboys* 1979

4. *Chinese Roulette* 1979

5. *Love Me to Death* 1980

6. *Killer Satellites* 1980

Bronson series

by Philip Rawls

published by Manor Books

Streets Of Blood 1975

Cherry Delight series

by Glen Chase

published by Leisure Books

Where The Action Is 1977

Kung Fu series featuring Mace

by Lee Chang

published by Manor Books

6. *The Year Of The Boar* 1975

Ryker series

by Nelson De Mille

published by Leisure Books

3. *The Terrorists* 1974

Super Cop Joe Blaze series

by Robert Novak

published by Belmont Tower Books

3. *The Thrill Killers* 1974

The Sharpshooter Series

by Bruno Rossi

published by Leisure Books

4. *The Worst Way to Die* 1974

5. *Night of the Assassins* 1974

7. *Headcrusher* 1974

NON-SERIES NOVELS

Those marked with *** have been republished as e-books under my real name, Len Levinson.

Those marked with ### have been republished in paperback under my real name, Len Levinson.

Cobra Woman by Len Levinson, first published by Rough Edges Press in 2019 ***###

Grip Of Death by Len Levinson, first published by Rough Edges Press in 2019 ***###

Web Of Doom by Len Levinson, first published by Rough Edges Press in 2018 ***###

Without Mercy by Leonard Jordan, Zebra 1981 ***###

The Goering Treasure by Gordon Davis, Zebra 1980 ***###

The Last Buffoon by Leonard Jordan, Belmont Tower 1980***###

Cabby by Leonard Jordan, Belmont Tower 1980

The Fast Life by Cynthia Wilkerson, Belmont Tower 1979***###

Doom Platoon by Richard Gallagher, Belmont Tower 1978 ***###

Sweeter Than Candy by Cynthia Wilkerson, Belmont Tower 1978

Inside Job by Nicholas Brady, Leisure 1978 ***###

Hype! by Leonard Jordan, Fawcett 1977***###

The Camp by Jonathan Trask, Belmont Tower 1977

The Bar Studs by Leonard Jordan, Fawcett 1976 ***###

Shark Fighter by Nicholas Brady, Belmont Tower 1975***###

Operation Perfidia by Leonard Jordan, Warner 1975 ***###

Private Sessions by March Hastings, Midwood 1974 (this was my first published novel, XXX rated hardcore erotica.)

---

83 novels published originally under 22 pseudonyms plus 3 published originally under my real name Len Levinson for grand total of 86.

A LOOK AT: TRIPLE THREAT

A LEN LEVINSON OMNIBUS

A MEANINGFUL COLLECTION OF MURDER MYSTERY AND HISTORICALLY MISMATCHED LOVE.

In *Web of Doom*, a former NYPD cop stumbles upon a murdered socialite. But when he reports the crime—as any good citizen should—detectives think he's to blame. Will this ex-cop solve the crime or do the time?

The Civil War is just beginning in *Grip of Death*, and someone is killing prominent Wall Street tycoons. Who's the culprit? Disgruntled investors, southern sympathizers hoping to destabilize the banking system, or Marxist revolutionaries?

Set in New York City in the 1980's, *Cobra Woman* is a romantic comedy about a Jewish-American advertising copywriter and a Cuban Catholic former-showgirl. Can they overcome their vast cultural differences and find true love?

Readers everywhere are sure to get lost in this immersive collection of murder, mystery, and obsessive love...

AVAILABLE NOW

ABOUT THE AUTHOR

Len Levinson is the author of 86 novels, published originally under a variety of pseudonyms by Bantam, Dell, Fawcett, Harper, Jove, Charter Diamond, Zebra, Belmont-Tower and Signet, among others. He has been acclaimed a "Trash Genius" by *Paperback Fanatic* magazine, and his books have sold an estimated two and a half million copies.

Len was born in 1935 in Massachusetts, enlisted in the Army at age 19, attended Michigan State University on the GI Bill and, after graduation with a B.A. in 1961, relocated to New York City where he worked in advertising and publicity for ten years before becoming a full-time novelist.

In 2003, after forty-two years in New York City, he relocated to a small town in Illinois—population 3000—surrounded by corn and soybean fields, a quiet and peaceful place for a writer. Len lives near four state forests, regularly hikes in one or the other and is a voracious reader of novels, history and biography.